Aquinas on Creation

Writings on the "Sentences" of Peter Lombard 2.1.1

Translated with an introduction and notes by

STEVEN E. BALDNER & WILLIAM E. CARROLL

The six articles that comprise Book 2, Distinction 1, Question 1 of Aquinas' *Writings on the "Sentences" of Peter Lombard* (*Scriptum super libros Sententiarum Petri Lombardi*) represent his earliest and most succinct account of creation. These texts contain the essential Thomistic doctrines on the subject, and are here translated into English for the first time, along with an introduction and analysis.

In Article One Aquinas argues, against Manichean dualism, that there is one ultimate cause of all created being; in so doing he gives three proofs for the existence of the Creator and the essential features of his answer to the problem of evil. Thomas establishes his definition of creation in Article Two, providing the needed distinctions between philosophical and theological senses of creation. Emanationism and the problem whether there can be any intermediary causes in God's act of creation are the subject of Article Three. The next article demonstrates that, although God is the cause of all created being, nevertheless creatures are true causes in nature.

Article Five argues that it is from revelation alone that we know that the world had a temporal beginning and that the philosophical arguments that purport to show either the necessity or impossibility of the temporal beginning are not persuasive. A detailed exposition of the meaning of the first sentence of the Bible, "In the beginning God created the heavens and the earth," follows in Article Six.

MEDIAEVAL SOURCES IN TRANSLATION 35

Aquinas on Creation

Writings on the "Sentences" of Peter Lombard

Book 2, Distinction 1, Question 1

*Translated with
an introduction and notes by*

STEVEN E. BALDNER

& WILLIAM E. CARROLL

PONTIFICAL INSTITUTE OF MEDIAEVAL STUDIES

Acknowledgments

This book has been published with a grant from the Humanities and Social Sciences Federation of Canada, using funds provided by the Social Sciences and Humanities Research Council of Canada.

Canadian Cataloguing in Publication Data

Thomas, Aquinas, Saint, 1225?–1274

    Aquinas on creation: Writings on the Sentences of Peter Lombard 2.1.1
(Mediaeval sources in translation, ISSN 0316-0874 ; 35)
Includes bibliographical references and index.
ISBN 0-88844-285-8

1. Peter Lombard, Bishop of Paris, ca. 1100–1160. Sententiarum libri IV.
2. Creation – Early works to 1800. 3. Catholic Church – Doctrines – Early
works to 1800. I. Baldner, Steven Earl, 1951– . II. Carroll, William E.
III. Pontifical Institute of Mediaeval Studies. IV. Title. V. Series.

BT695.T46 1997   231.7'65   C97-932241-3

Pontifical Institute of Mediaeval Studies
59 Queen's Park Crescent East
Toronto, Ontario, Canada M5S 2C4

Printed in Canada

To the memory of
Father James A. Weisheipl, OP,
our teacher and friend

Contents

Preface

Explanations of the origin of the universe have fascinated men and women in every age. The distinctively Christian doctrine of creation out of nothing received its fullest expression and most sophisticated exposition in the thirteenth century at the hands of St. Thomas Aquinas. The doctrine of creation represents a crucial nexus of faith and reason. Is there common ground, for example, between the believer's claim that the world was created out of nothing and the natural scientist's insistence that it is impossible to get something from nothing? Must one choose between the conclusions of reason and the tenets of faith? The discussion of such topics in the Middle Ages – by Muslims, Jews, and Christians – was profound. Aquinas, himself, recognized a considerable debt to Muslim and Jewish thinkers.

The text on creation we have translated, a section from Aquinas' *Writings on the "Sentences" of Peter Lombard*, has never been published in English. It is the most economical of Aquinas' extensive accounts of creation, and yet it contains the basis of all his future commentary on the subject. It is a rich work, worthy of analysis in its own right as well as for understanding Aquinas' place in the history of reflection on creation. The distinctions Aquinas draws among physics (natural philosophy), metaphysics, and theology have much to offer contemporary discourse concerning cosmology and creation. Most importantly, we think that what Aquinas says about creation is true.

We have provided a brief historical introduction to the development of the doctrine of creation (to Aquinas) and we have provided an analysis of the translated text itself. The text is not always easy to understand and we hope that the summary found in our analysis will assist readers. The appendices include supplementary material: a selection from the *Summa theologiae* in which Aquinas rejects emanationism as philosophically possible; a new translation of *De aeternitate*

selection from the *Summa theologiae* in which Aquinas rejects emana-tionism as philosophically possible; a new translation of *De aeternitate mundi* (*On the Eternity of the World*), which is Aquinas' most mature work on the question of creation and the eternity of the world; selec-tions from Aquinas' *Commentary* on Aristotle's *Physics*, in which Aquinas rejects Aristotle's arguments for the eternity of the world; a brief selection of texts in which Aquinas attributes to Aristotle a doc-trine of creation; a translation of the prologue of the second book of Aquinas' *Writings on the "Sentences"* in which our principal text is found; and a glossary of important terms found in the text we have translated. Unless specified otherwise, all translations are our own.

We should like to thank the Earhart Foundation for a generous grant which made this volume possible. Its preparation began in the late 1970s when a group of graduate students and professors met at the Pontifical Institute for Mediaeval Studies (Toronto) to discuss this text. As participants in this year-long undertaking we benefitted from the insightful comments of many collaborators. Above all, however, we are grateful to the late Father James Weisheipl, who led these discus-sions and whose own analysis of Aquinas and medieval natural philo-sophy, metaphysics, and theology has contributed substantially to our work. We are also grateful for the expert editorial assistance provided by Fred Unwalla of the Pontifical Institute of Mediaeval Studies and also for the work of Andrew Holm and Christian Hellie in the prepara-tion of the final text of the index.

Introduction

In principio: An Introduction to Creation *ex nihilo*

Origins of the Doctrine

If one were to read the opening line of Genesis without any reference to the history of Christian thought, it would not be immediately apparent that the words, "In the beginning God created the heavens and the earth," are an affirmation of creation out of nothing. In fact, there continues to be considerable disagreement as to how the opening verse of the Bible ought to be understood. Some scholars translate the first verse as "In the beginning when God created the heavens and the earth, the earth was without form and void." Such a rendering of the original Hebrew text would certainly seem to call into question an explicit source in Genesis for the doctrine of creation out of nothing.[1]

The opening of Genesis is not the earliest text in the Bible. It received its final written form only during the period of the Babylonian exile of the Jewish people. The prophets of Israel remind the Jews, in the midst of their pessimism, that their God is not like other gods. God who has made a covenant with Abraham and who brought His

---

1. The Latin Vulgate's text is: *In principio creavit Deus caelum et terram.* The King James text from the early seventeenth century is: "In the beginning God created the heaven and the earth." The French Jerusalem Bible in the twentieth century has a similar rendering: "Au commencement, Dieu créa le ciel et la terre." Yet, the New English Bible, also in the twentieth century, is quite different: "In the beginning of creation, when God made heaven and earth, the earth was without form and void, with darkness over the face of the abyss, and a mighty wind that swept over the surface of the waters." Hebrew scholars are not unanimous in how one ought to translate the Hebrew *bara'* – the word which becomes *creavit* in Latin. For a recent study of the various ways the opening of Genesis can be understood, see Bruce Vawter's essay on Genesis in *A New Catholic Commentary on Holy Scripture*, gen. ed. Reginald C. Fuller (New York: Thomas Nelson, 1969), pp. 172–174 (148a–h).

people out of Egypt is the Creator of all that is.[2] Hebrew scriptures return, from time to time, to this theme. Indeed, immediately following the initial account of creation in Genesis there is a second story of origins, a story composed before the first and containing different imagery. We can find other commentary in the Psalms and in the Wisdom literature. Throughout the Bible there are various images and modes of speaking which bear witness to the fundamental truth of God's creative act.

The question of reading the opening line of Genesis – aside from identifying what the line is – is part of a much larger question: how does one read the Bible? When we look at the development of the Christian doctrine of creation we must remember how Christians in the early Church and in the Middle Ages approached the *evidence* from biblical revelation. They read Genesis, for example, not as an isolated account of origins, but as part of a whole, which could be understood only with Christ in mind. Thus, for example, Christians read the opening of Genesis in the light of the opening of the Gospel of John: identifying "in the beginning" with "in/through Christ."[3]

2. "It was in exile and in the seeming defeat of Israel that there occurred an opening to the awareness of the God who holds every people and all of history in His hands, who holds everything because He is the Creator of everything and the source of all power" (Cardinal Joseph Ratzinger, *'In the Beginning ...': A Catholic Understanding of the Story of Creation and the Fall*, trans. Boniface Ramsey [Grand Rapids, MI: W.B. Eerdmans, 1995], pp. 11–12.)

3. Ibid., pp. 9–10. The Gospel of John opens with the words: "In the beginning was the Word. ..." Robert Alter, a leading literary scholar of the Hebrew Scriptures, argues that the "atomistic" tendency to discover "discontinuities, contradictions, duplications, and fissures" in the text of the Bible, has drawn our attention away from the design of the whole. The Hebrew Bible, he writes, "is a corpus which bears within it the seeds of its own canonicity." It is "a set of texts in restless dialogue with one another." Alter observes that "the stark initiating act of creation through divine speech from formlessness, chaos, nothingness (*tohu-bohu*) lingers in the Hebrew imagination as a measure of the absoluteness of God's power and also as a looming perspective on the contingency of all human existence and the frailty of all human exercises of knowledge and power. ... Sometime in the latter part of the second millennium BCE, the spiritual avant-garde of the Hebrew people began to imagine creation and Creator, history and humankind, in a radically new way. This radicalism of vision, though it would never produce anything like unanimity, generated certain underlying patterns of literary expression in the centuries that followed" (*The Literary Guide to the Bible*, ed. Alter and Frank Kermode [Cambridge, MA: Harvard University Press, 1987], pp. 25, 31, 34). Other excellent books by Alter

Beginning in the sixteenth century, in part as a result of the controversies of the Reformation, the living unity of Scripture was subordinated to a kind of *propositionalization* according to which each text, each verse, was read in its bare literalness. Such literalism (as distinct from the literal meaning of the Bible)[4] was evident in the dispute between the Inquisition and Galileo. In the twentieth century, the concern for the biblical text as a historical document – connected with the times and culture in which it was composed – often excludes the consideration of how each text is an integral part of the Bible as a whole. Such an approach to the Bible leads many to question whether the opening line of Genesis can really support the doctrine of creation out of nothing.[5]

It is important to recognize a distinction between creation, understood as God's causing the universe to be, and the account of the "six days of creation" set forth in Genesis. As Augustine and Aquinas observe, what is essential to the Christian faith is the fact of creation, not

---

are: *The Art of Biblical Narrative* (1981); *The Art of Biblical Poetry* (1985); and *The World of Biblical Literature* (1992). Still one of the best accounts of medieval exegesis is: Beryl Smalley, *The Study of the Bible in the Middle Ages* (Oxford: Basil Blackwell, 1952; reptd. Notre Dame, IN: University of Notre Dame Press, 1964).

4. In the theological tradition of biblical interpretation, the literal sense of Sacred Scripture is what the author (i.e., ultimately God) intends the words to mean. The literal sense is, thus, quite distinct from a *literalistic* emphasis on the bare signification of the words. A common example is Scripture's reference to God's stretching out His hand. The literal sense of this passage refers to God's power, not to some divine anatomical part. For a current discussion of the Catholic understanding of biblical interpretation see the 1993 report of the Pontifical Biblical Commission: Joseph A. Fitzmyer, *The Biblical Commission's Document 'The Interpretation of the Bible in the Church': Text and Commentary* (Rome: Editrice Pontificio Istituto Biblico, 1995). For a brief history of the interpretation of the creation stories in Genesis, see Frank Egleston Robbins, *The Hexaemeral Literature: A Study of the Greek and Latin Commentaries on Genesis* (Chicago: University of Chicago Press, 1912).

5. The new historical thinking "no longer read the texts forward but backward – that is, with a view not to Christ but to the probable origins of those texts. People were no longer concerned with understanding what a text said or what a thing was from the aspect of its fulfillment, but from that of its beginning, its source. As a result of this isolation from the whole and of this literal-mindedness with respect to particulars, which contradicts the entire inner nature of the Bible but which was now considered to be the truly scientific approach, there arose that conflict between the natural sciences and theology which has been, up to our own day, a burden for the faith" (Ratzinger, *'In the Beginning,'* p. 17). Robert Alter speaks of an "atomistic" approach to the text; see n3 above.

its manner or mode.[6] The explanation of the six days is really an account of the *formation* of the world, not its *creation*. Such explanations, given by Patristic and medieval thinkers in their hexaemeral literature, involved a commentary on Genesis rather than a philosophical treatment of creation. Often in this hexaemeral literature we find elaborate attempts to discover a concordance between the description of the formation of the world and contemporary scientific knowledge of the world. On the other hand, the philosophical and theological treatment of creation is the investigation of the dependence of all that is on God. In the language of metaphysics, creation is a dependence in the order of being. Thus questions such as, how does the first cause give being (existence) to creatures, and how do creatures receive the being that is given to them, are central to such an investigation. Although the problem of creation may well have entered philosophical discourse because of a belief in God's revelation, it is nevertheless a problem that can be, and was in the Middle Ages, treated in a properly philosophical way. In fact, the discussion of creation is an excellent example of the ways in which medieval thinkers in diverse religious traditions wrestled with the relationship between faith and reason, and between theology and philosophy.

In the early Church, well before the thirteenth century and the age of Thomas Aquinas, there was little question among Christian thinkers that Genesis did reveal that God created the world out of nothing. The encounter between the biblical affirmation of the radical dependence of all things upon God as their source and the traditions of Western philosophical and scientific reflection constitutes one of the central characteristics of Western culture. Although the origins of the Christian understanding of creation are prior to philosophical and theologi-

---

6. "There are some things that are by their very nature the substance of the faith, as to say of God that He is three and one ... about which it is forbidden for anyone to think otherwise. ... There are other things that relate to the faith only incidentally ... and, with respect to these, Christian authors have different opinions, interpreting the Sacred Scripture in various ways. Thus with respect to the origin of the world, there is one point that is of the substance of faith, viz., to know that it began by creation. ... But the manner and the order according to which creation took place concerns the faith only incidentally ..." (Aquinas, *In 2 Sent.* 12.3.1; see also *De potentia Dei* 4. 2). Aquinas' commentary on the story of creation in Genesis can be found in *Summa theologiae* 1. 65–74.

cal reflection,[7] it is in the encounter between philosophy and science, on the one hand, and the insights derived from Scripture, on the other, that the Christian *doctrine* of creation is forged. We need to remember that doctrines, even Church doctrines, have their origins in time, place, and historical circumstance. Such rootedness in history does not invalidate claims for a truth of doctrine transcending time and place, but it does mean that as we seek to understand the doctrine – a task which is both theological and philosophical – we need the assistance of history.

When theologians in the second, third, and fourth centuries came to define the Christian view of nature, human nature, and God – as distinct from the views found in the pagan intellectual world in which they lived – they found in the opening verses of Genesis, interpreted in the light of Christian faith, a source for a view of creation they developed into a doctrine of the origin of the universe characteristically their own. The Hellenistic world in which the early Christian theologians sought to understand their faith shared an intellectual patrimony which, despite its diversity, maintained that the universe is eternal. From Heraclitus and Parmenides to Plato and Aristotle, and from the Stoics to Plotinus, the ancient philosophers appeared to speak with one voice. Whether there be nothing but change or change be an illusion, whether we distinguish between a world of becoming and a world of being, or between potentiality and actuality, one thing is clear: there is no absolute temporal beginning of the universe. For the Church Fathers, Christian revelation stood out in stark contrast to this traditional philosophical view. Despite an early flirtation with a Platonic interpretation, according to which God forms the world in the same way as does Plato's Demiurge in the *Timaeus*, by the early second century we discover the first clear indications of what becomes the orthodox doctrine of creation out of nothing.[8]

---

7. The doctrine of creation out of nothing did not receive its first *formulation* in Jewish theology in the Hellenistic age. Although some Jewish theologians did speak of God's creating "out of nothing," recent scholarship has shown that the famous passage from 2 Maccabees 7:28, for instance, was not meant in a metaphysical sense and did not exclude God's working with existent matter; see Georg Shmuttermayr, "'Shöpfung aus dem Nichts' in 2 Makk. 7:28?: Zum Verhältnis von Position und Bedeutung," *Biblische Zeitschrift*, neue folge 17 (1973): 203–228.

8. For an excellent survey of this development see Gerhard May, '*Creatio ex nihilo': The Doctrine of 'Creation out of Nothing' in Early Christian Thought*, trans. A.S. Worrall (Edinburgh: T. and T. Clark, 1994).

By the early third century (*ca.* 230) Hippolytus of Rome, in a sustained polemic entitled, *The Refutation of All Heresies*, offers a clear, concise statement of the Christian doctrine of creation:

> The one God, the first and only Deity, both Creator and Lord of all, had nothing coeval with Himself, not infinite chaos, nor measureless water or solid earth, nor dense air, not warm fire, nor refined spirit, nor the azure canopy of the stupendous firmament. But He was One, alone in Himself. By an exercise of His will He created things that are, which antecedently had no existence, except that He willed to make them.[9]

The God in whom Christians believe is transcendent – wholly other than the world. He is not on the same ontological level – i.e., the same level of being – with any thing. In order to affirm the transcendence of the Christian God one must affirm a radical distinction between God and the universe, a distinction which the Church Fathers were convinced was denied in the Hellenistic view that the world is eternal. The God of Abraham, the God who reveals Himself as "I Am Who Am," cannot be co-eternal with anything else. For the Church Fathers, to claim that the world is eternal is to claim that it is equal to God. Thus, one important reason for making clear that Christians believe in a God who creates the world out of nothing is to deny any kind of identification of the world with God. Not even eternal formless stuff which a demiurgic god molds or forms into the created universe is acceptable: God must be Creator of all, including formless matter.

Only God is eternal; the world is finite. We see in the early discussion of the Christian doctrine of creation the equating of the temporally finite with the created, and of the eternal with the uncreated. Later commentators, Christian, Jewish, and Muslim, will argue, in addition, that an eternal universe is a necessary universe: necessary in the sense that such a universe would be wholly self-sufficient, with no need for a cause, or necessary in the sense that it would not be the production of God's will. A necessary universe could not be a universe

---

9. Hippolytus, *Refutatio omnium haeresium* 10.32, ed. Miroslav Marcovich, (Berlin and New York: Walter de Gruyter, 1986), pp. 408–409; trans. As *The Refutation of All Heresies* in *The Ante-Nicene Fathers*, ed. Alexander Roberts and James Donaldson, 9 vols. (Buffalo: Christian Literature Co., 1885–1903), 5: 150 (translation modified).

which depended upon the free creative act of God. In order to defend a view of God as absolutely free and sovereign, it seemed that one must affirm that the world is temporally finite. Although it is true that a world which is temporally finite (in which, that is, there is a t=0) is a world produced by the will of another, there will be considerable debate as to whether the world must have a temporal beginning if it is in fact the result of God's choice. Again, if the universe has an absolute beginning, before[10] which it was not, then its coming-into-existence requires a divine agent. The question which will occupy our attention when we turn to Aquinas and the thirteenth century is: if the world is created by God, *must* it have a temporal beginning, i.e., must it be temporally finite? Even the view of Plotinus (203/4–269/70), who reduces the source of all to a divine One, fails for Christians to recognize the radical freedom of divine creation. Creation as a free act must be distinct from any form of necessary emanation, i.e., of a divine "bubbling over" of being.

Furthermore, for the Church Fathers, the view that the world is eternal, in the specific sense of being without a finite temporal duration, seemed inevitably to require a cyclical view of history, a view that would raise fundamental problems for Christianity. Only a temporally finite world could constitute the scene for the religious drama of Fall and Redemption, with its central, unique, unrepeatable event: the coming of Christ. Only in a world temporally finite did it seem possible to make sense of the Christian understanding of each man's destiny providentially designed by a loving God. If salvation history is to make sense, time cannot be cyclical.

Among the Church Fathers, Saint Augustine (354–430) makes the most important contribution to the doctrine of creation. His sustained explication of the account of creation found in Genesis[11] served as the foundation for future Christian commentary on the subject. Not only does he make clear the difference between an eternal universe of Greek

---

10. Obviously the sense of "before" the beginning of time involves an act of imagination since there can be no temporal "before" before there is time. We will see Aquinas make this point.

11. For an account of Augustine's understanding of creation, see Ernan McMullin, "Introduction," in *Evolution and Creation*, ed. Ernan McMullin (University of Notre Dame Press, 1985), pp. 9–16. See also Etienne Gilson, *The Christian Philosophy of St. Augustine*, trans. L.E.M. Lynch (London: Victor Gollancz, 1961), pp. 189–196.

philosophy and the Christian understanding that the universe and time begin together, but he also distinguishes between the way we come to know creatures as they exist and develop in time and the way God knows creatures as their cause. Augustine observes that there are "two moments of creation":

> one in the original creation when God made all creatures before resting from all His works on the seventh day, and the other in the administration of creatures by which He works even now. In the first instance God made everything together without any moments of time intervening, but now He works within the course of time, by which we see the stars move from their rising to their setting, the weather change from summer to winter ... .[12]

When we think of the first creation we should not think of God's activity as occurring over a period of "solar days" as though God works in time. The creation in Genesis occurred simultaneously: "He made that which gave time its beginning, as He made all things together, disposing them in an order based not on intervals of time but on causal connections."[13]

Augustine also recognizes that God's creative agency is not only exercised at the beginning of the universe, but continuously, causing all that is to exist.

> For the power and might of the Creator, who rules and embraces all, makes every creature abide; and if this power ever ceases to govern creatures, their essences would pass away and all nature would perish. When a builder puts up a house and departs, his work remains in spite of the fact that he is no longer there. But the universe will pass away in the twinkling of an eye if God withdraws His ruling hand. ...
>
> We must, therefore, distinguish in the works of God those which He makes even now and those from which He rested on

12. Augustine, *De Genesi ad litterarm* 5.11.27; trans. John Hammond Taylor as *The Literal Meaning of Genesis*, Ancient Christian Writers 41–42, 2 vols. (New York: Newman Press, 1982), 1: 162.

13. Ibid., 5.5.12; trans. Taylor, 1: 154.

the seventh day. For there are some who think that only the world was made by God and that everything else is made by the world according to His ordination and command, but that God Himself makes nothing [other than His original act of creation]. ... Hence, God moves His whole creation by a hidden power, and all creatures are subject to this movement: the angels carry out His commands, the stars move in their courses, the winds blow now this way, now that, deep pools seethe with tumbling waterfalls and mists forming above them, meadows come to life as their seeds put forth the grass, animals are born and live their lives according to their proper instincts, the evil are permitted to try the just. It is thus that God unfolds the generations which He laid up in creation when first He founded it; and they would not be sent forth to run their course if He who made creatures ceased to exercise His provident rule over them.[14]

Although strongly influenced by Neoplatonic thought, Augustine thinks there is a significant gulf between classical culture and biblical revelation on the origin of the world and the kind of causality which the Creator exercises. One scholar has noted that for Saint Augustine it was precisely with respect to the eternity or non-eternity of the world that we find the frontier between paganism and Christianity.[15]

Another reason underlying the commitment of the Church Fathers to the doctrine of creation out of nothing was the necessity of rejecting every temptation to identify matter or the world with evil. To protect God from being the author of evil, some thinkers were ready to accuse matter. If matter is evil, it must not be dependent upon God; it must not be created; it must be eternal. The arguments were varied, but

---

14. Ibid., 4.12.22; trans. Taylor 1: 117; and 5.20.40–41; trans. Taylor 1:171–172.

15. "Au IVᵉ siècle après Jésus Christ, le problème de l'éternité du monde touche presque à tous les autres: tout y est de quelque manière impliqué: la béatitude de l'âme et la réalité du mal, la solidité du monde physique et la signification de l'histoire, les attributs et la science de Dieu, la rationalité de la religion de l'Evangile, l'éternité de Rome, la fidélité à César. Saint Augustin pouvait se représenter avec maladresse la nature exacte de son différend avec les platoniciens: il ne se trompait pourtant pas en pensant que la question de l'éternité du monde jalonnait leur frontière" (Jean Guitton, *Le temps et l'éternité chez Plotin et Saint Augustin*, 4th ed. [Paris: Vrin, 1971], p. 207).

from the Marcionites to the Manichees to the Gnostics, the claim was essentially the same: matter is evil. The Gnostics experienced the physical universe as a hostile, fragile place, hardly attributable to the creative act of the true God: rather, it must be the work of heavenly beings of lower rank and limited power, who did not know the true God or rebelled against Him. For the Gnostics, the problem of the origin of evil is ultimately inseparable from the question of the origin of the universe.[16] The Manichees were radical dualists: the spiritual world, including the human soul, is created by God, the principle of all good; the material world, including the human body, is created by the evil principle. In contradistinction to such views, the doctrine of creation captures the core of the Christian faith: God alone is the source of all that is; He brings everything, including matter, into existence; all that He creates is good. It is Augustine who, in the late fourth century, provides the classic response to the problem of evil while affirming the goodness of all that is. His exposition of evil as privation is, of course, another story; the point to re-emphasize here is that the doctrine of creation out of nothing, forged in the early centuries of Christian history, served to distinguish what Christians believed about the ultimate origin and goodness of the world, from Hellenistic philosophy, from Gnosticism, and from Manicheanism. At least in these early centuries Christian thinkers were convinced that there was a fundamental incompatibility between the pagan affirmation of an eternal universe and Christian faith in creation: therefore, for them, to affirm that the universe is created by God necessarily means to deny that the universe is eternal.

The classical philosophical argument for the eternity of the world received an important challenge in the sixth century when, in Alexandria (Egypt), John Philoponus responded to attacks on the Christian belief that the universe had a beginning, found in the writings of Proclus (*ca.* 411–485), the famous head of the Neoplatonic Academy in

16. See May, '*Creatio ex nihilo*,' pp. 39–61, at p. 51: "The doctrine of the creation of the world by angelic powers seems to belong to an earlier stage of gnosticism. Only later is the God of the Old Testament distinguished from the highest God and seen as the actual Creator of the world, while the demiurgical function of the angels recedes." Marcion, for example, urges a radical distinction between the God of the Old Testament and the God of the New Testament. The Creator-god of the Old Testament fashioned the world out of eternal matter, a matter "bad and hateful" (pp. 58–59).

Athens. Proclus, it seemed, had argued that although the present orderly arrangement of the universe might have had a beginning, still it was absurd to think that matter itself had a beginning. Proclus suggested that one may conceive of a succession, indeed an endless succession, of worlds. In *De aeternitate mundi contra Proclum*, written in 529,[17] Philoponus not only restates the Christian doctrine of an absolute temporal beginning to the universe; he also argues that on philosophical (i.e., scientific in the broadest sense) grounds one must conclude that the universe is temporally finite. This treatise represents a significant shift in the history of the doctrine of creation out of nothing, for Philoponus contends that on the basis of the principles of Greek thought, especially Aristotle's arguments for the impossibility of an actual infinity, one knows for sure that the universe could not be eternal. Philoponus points out that were the universe to be infinite there would have to be an actual infinity of past days. Furthermore, if past days were infinite, what sense could one make of adding today to this past series, since one cannot increase the infinite? Philoponus was convinced that he had "found a contradiction at the heart of paganism, a contradiction between their concept of infinity and their denial of a beginning."[18] Although Philoponus remained more or less unknown in the Latin Middle Ages, the arguments he advanced can be found in texts of many medieval Islamic, Jewish, and Christian thinkers. As we shall see, Thomas Aquinas subjects these arguments to a trenchant analysis.

17. Richard Sorabji points out that "529 was an *annus mirabilis* for Christianity. St. Benedict, on the usual dating, founded the monastery at Monte Cassino, the Council of Orange settled outstanding matters on free will, Justinian [the Christian Emperor] closed the Neoplatonist school at Athens, and Philoponus produced his book of eighteen arguments 'On the Eternity of the World Against the Neoplatonist Proclus'" ("Infinity and the Creation," in *Philoponus and the Rejection of Aristotelian Science*, ed. Sorabji [Ithaca, NY: Cornell University Press, 1987], pp. 164–178, at p. 167). See also, *Philoponus: Against Aristotle on the Eternity of the World*, trans. Christian Wildberg (Ithaca: Cornell University Press, 1987).

18. Sorabji, "Infinity and the Creation," p. 177. Sorabji has written two books of particular importance for the understanding of creation in the light of traditional philosophical reflection: *Time Creation, and the Continuum* (Ithaca: Cornell University Press, 1983) and *Matter, Space, and Motion: Theories in Antiquity and Their Sequel* (Ithaca: Cornell University Press, 1988).

Creation in Avicenna, Averroes, and Maimonides[19]

Aquinas' development of his understanding of creation depends heavily upon the work of medieval Muslim and Jewish thinkers. The reception of Greek philosophy in the Islamic world is a complex story. As early as 932 there was a famous public debate in Baghdad over the merits of the "new learning."[20] Greek philosophy seemed particularly challenging to many *mutakallimun* (theologians) who came to view it with suspicion as an alien way of thinking. The work of al-Fārābī (870–950), who established in Cairo a curriculum for the study of Plato and Aristotle, and of Avicenna (980–1037), whose writings in medicine, natural philosophy, and metaphysics proved to be extraordinarily influential, offers an excellent example of the way in which Greek thought was appropriated in the Islamic world.[21] Avicenna, translated into Latin, will prove to be especially important for Thomas Aquinas, as we shall see. Avicenna's understanding of the relationship between God, the absolutely necessary being, and the created order of things which are, in themselves, only possible will contribute to Aquinas' understanding of creation. In his monumental *al-Shifā': al-Ilāhiyyāt*, Avicenna writes: "This is what it means that a thing is created, that is, receiving its existence from another ... . As a result everything, in rela-

---

19. Throughout, we have used Latinized versions of the names of Muslim and Jewish thinkers such as Ibn Sīnā, Ibn Rushd, and Moses ben Maimon, since our primary concern is the influence they had on Aquinas, and Aquinas read them in Latin translations.

20. See Oliver Leaman, *An Introduction to Medieval Islamic Philosophy* (Cambridge University Press, 1985); Herbert A. Davidson, *Proofs for Eternity, Creation and the Existence of God in Medieval Islamic and Jewish Philosophy* (New York: Oxford University Press, 1987); Fadlou Shehadi, *Metaphysics in Islamic Philosophy* (Delmar, NY: Caravan Books, 1982); and Edward Booth, *Aristotelian Aporetic Ontology in Islamic and Christian Thinkers.* (Cambridge: Cambridge University Press, 1983). The specific debate concerned whether Aristotelian logic transcended the Greek language and was, thus, appropriate to use by those who spoke and wrote in Arabic: see Shehadi, *Metaphysics in Islamic Philosophy,* pp. 23–24.

21. On al-Fārābī, see Ian R. Netton, *Al-Fārābī and His School* (London and New York: Routledge, 1992). An excellent survey of Avicenna, by several authors and on a range of topics, can be found in the article in *Encyclopaedia Iranica* (London and New York: Routledge & Kegan Paul, 1989), 3: 66–110. Also see Lenn E. Goodman, *Avicenna* (London and New York: Routledge, 1992).

tion to the first cause, is created. ... Therefore, every single thing, except the primal One, exists after not having existed with respect to itself."[22]

> When some thing through its own essence is continuously a cause for the existence of some other thing, it is a cause for it continuously as long as its essence continues existing. If it [the cause] exists continuously, then that which is caused exists continuously. Thus, what is like this [cause] is among the highest causes, for it prevents the non-existence of something, and is that which gives perfect existence to something. This is the meaning of that which is called 'creation' [ibda'] by the philosophers, namely, the bringing into existence of something after absolute non-existence. For it belongs to that which is caused, in itself, that it does not exist [laysa], while it belongs to it from its cause that it does exist [aysa]. That which belongs to something in itself is prior, according to the mind, in essence, not in time to that which comes from another. Thus, everything which is caused is existing after non-existing by a posteriority in terms of essence. ... If [an effect's] existence comes after an absolute non-existence, its emanation from the cause in this way is called ibda' ("absolute origination"). This is the most excellent form of the bestowal of existence, for (in this case) non-existence has simply been prevented and existence has been given the sway ab initio.[23]

In explaining the kind of efficient causality which creation involves, Avicenna notes that there is an important difference between

22. al-Shifā': al-Ilāhiyyāt 8.3, trans. Georges Anawati, La Métaphysique du Shifā', 2 vols. (Paris: Vrin, 1978), 2: 83–84: "C'est ce qui veut dire que la chose est créé, i.e., recevant l'existence d'un autre. ... Par conséquent le tout par rapport à la Cause première est créé. ... Donc toute chose, sauf l'Un premier, existe après n'avoir par existé eu égard à elle-même [bistihqaq nafsihi]."
23. al-Shifā': al-Ilāhiyyāt 6.2, trans. Anawati, Métaphysique du Shifā' 2: 266–267. The translation here conflates the versions made by Barry S. Kogan, Averroes and the Metaphysics of Causation (Binghamton, NY: State University of New York Press, 1985), p. 276, n58, and Fazhur Rahman, "Ibn Sīnā's Theory of the God-World Relationship," in God and Creation: An Ecumenical Symposium, ed. David B. Burrell and Bernard McGinn (Notre Dame, IN: University of Notre Dame Press, 1990), pp. 38–52, at pp. 41–42, n5.

the ways in which metaphysicians and natural philosophers discuss efficient cause: "... the metaphysicians do not intend by the agent the principle of movement only, as do the natural philosophers, but also the principle of existence and that which bestows [existence], such as the Creator of the world."[24]

The recognition that creation is properly a subject of metaphysics and not of physics (i.e., of natural philosophy) will be particularly important for Aquinas, as will Avicenna's insistence on the distinction between essence and existence. With respect to the latter topic, Avicenna observes that a reflection on what it means for something to be reveals that what something is – i.e., its essence – is different from whether a thing exists. On the basis of the ontological distinction between essence and existence, Avicenna argues that all beings other than God (in whom this distinction disappears) require a cause in order to exist.[25]

Avicenna's distinction between existence and essence is part of his contribution to a long standing intellectual project which sought to understand the relationship between existing individuals and their "intelligible natures." Those schooled in the Neoplatonic tradition gave ontological priority to the intelligible nature; hence, the attraction of an emanationist scheme according to which all existing things flow from a primal source of being and intelligibility. The immediate context of Avicenna's distinction is his discussion of necessary and possible being. Aquinas follows Avicenna's lead but comes to recognize a rather different sort of creaturely contingence from that of Avicenna. For Avicenna, essence is something prior and to which existence "happens" or comes as an accident.[26] According to Avicenna, "real

24. *al-Shifā': al-Ilāhiyyāt* 6.1, as translated by Arthur Hyman and James Walsh in their anthology *Philosophy in the Middle Ages: The Christian, Islamic, and Jewish Traditions,* 2nd ed. (Indianapolis: Hackett, 1987), p. 248.

25. "Il n'y a donc pas d'autre quiddité (*mahiyya*) pour le nécessairement existant que le fait qu'il est nécessairement existant. Et c'est cela l'être (*al-anniyya*)." *al-Shifā': al-Ilāhiyyāt* 8.4, trans. Anawati, *Métaphysique du Shifa'* 2: 87. The classic work on Avicenna's analysis of essence and existence is Amélie-Marie Goichon, *La distinction de l'essence et l'existence d'après Ibn Sīnā (Avicenne)* (Paris: Desclée de Brouwer, 1937).

26. David B. Burrell, "Aquinas and Islamic and Jewish Thinkers," in *The Cambridge Companion to Aquinas,* ed. Norman Kretzmann and Eleonore Stump (Cambridge: Cambridge University Press, 1993), pp. 60–84, at p. 69. In his introduction to

existence" emerges as a new attribute for the contingent being of the created world (which was originally present as an essence or "possibility" in the divine mind); it is "a kind of added benefit bestowed by God upon possible beings in the act of creation."[27] As David Burrell observes, Aquinas will use Avicenna's distinction between essence and existence but develop the notion of radical dependency in such a way that creaturely existence is understood not as something which happens to essence but as a fundamental *relation* to the Creator as origin.[28]

An eternal world, as we have seen, was often viewed as a necessary world. Avicenna sought to be faithful to Greek metaphysics (especially in the Neoplatonic tradition) and also to affirm the contingency of the created order.[29] Although the world proceeds from God by necessity and is eternal, it differs fundamentally from God in

---

the *Shifa'*, Anawati puts it this way: "C'est en partant de l'essence qu'Avicenne aboutit forcément à considérer l'*esse* qui l'affecte comme un accident. S. Thomas par contre part de l'être existant et il fait de l'*esse* ce qu'il y a de plus intime et de plus profond dans cet être" (*Métaphysique du Shifa,'* 1: 78). For an extensive discussion of the "accidentality of existence" in Avicenna, see Shehadi, *Metaphysics in Islamic Philosophy*, pp. 93–114.

27. Charles H. Kahn, "Why Existence Does Not Emerge as a Distinct Concept in Greek Philosophy," in *Philosophies of Existence: Ancient and Medieval*, ed. by Parviz Morewedge (Bronx, NY: Fordham University Press, 1982), pp. 7–17, at p. 8.

28. "In one fell swoop, Aquinas has succeeded in restoring the primacy Aristotle intended for individual existing things, by linking them directly to their Creator and by granting Avicenna's 'distinction' an unequivocal ontological status. Yet as should be clear, this is more than a development of Avicenna; it is a fresh start requiring a conception of *existing* that could no longer be confused with an *accident*, and which has the capacity to link each creature to the gratuitous activity of a free Creator. Only in such a way can the radical *newness* (*hudûth*) of the created universe find coherent expression, for the *existing* 'received from God' will be the source of all perfections and need not presume anything at all – be it matter or 'possibles'" (Burrell, "Aquinas and Islamic and Jewish Thinkers," pp. 69–70).

29. Avicenna, in his philosophic argumentation, "fused the Aristotelian metaphysics of self-sufficiency with the monotheistic metaphysics of contingency. ... The key to Ibn Sīnā's synthesis of contingency with the metaphysics of necessity lies in the single phrase: *considered in itself*. Considered in itself, each effect is radically contingent. It does not contain the conditions of its own existence; and, considered in itself, it need not exist. ... But considered in relation to its causes, not as something that in the abstract might never have existed, but as something concretely given before us. ... considered in relation to its causes, this object must exist, in the very Aristotelian sense that it does exist, and must have the nature that it has in that its causes gave it that nature" (Goodman, *Avicenna*, pp. 63, 66–67).

that *in itself* it is only possible and requires a cause in order to exist. God, on the other hand, is necessary in Himself and, thus, requires no cause. A key to science, in the sense set forth by Aristotle in his *Posterior Analytics*, is the knowledge of a necessary nexus between cause and effect; only such necessary knowledge truly deserves the name science (*episteme*). Contingent existence, although not necessary in itself (*per se*), is necessary through/by another.[30] Avicenna thought that the contingency of the world he described did not deny natural necessity.[31] A world without necessary relationships is an unintelligible world. Yet, at the same time, the fear was that a necessary world is a self-sufficient world, a world which cannot not be: the opposite, so it seemed, of a world created by God. At best a necessary world would only be a world which *must* surge forth from a primal source of being. The explanation of the absolute origin of the world in terms of a necessary emanationist schema was attractive since it seems to do justice to both necessity and dependence. Creation for Avicenna is an ontological relationship – a relationship in the order of being – with no reference to temporality. In fact, Avicenna accepted the established Greek view that the universe is eternal. Obviously, his view of the emanation of existing things from a primal source – a view which excluded the free act of God – only made sense in an eternal universe. But, does an emanationist metaphysics do justice to creation? Is it consistent with the God revealed in the Koran or the Bible?

It was precisely such questions which led al-Ghazālī (1058–1111), a jurist, theologian, and mystic, to argue against what he considered to be threats to Islam in the thought of philosophers such as Avicenna. In *The Incoherence of the Philosophers* [*Tahāfut al-Falāsifah*] al-Ghazālī sets forth a wide-ranging critique of Greek thought and defends what he considers to be the orthodox Islamic doctrine of creation versus Avicenna's embrace of an eternal world. Such a world, al-Ghazālī

30. See Emil I. Fackenheim, "The Possibility of the Universe in Al-Fārābī, Ibn Sīnā, and Maimonides," *Proceedings of the American Academy of Jewish Research* 16 (1947): 39–70; George F. Hourani, "Ibn Sīnā on Necessary and Possible Existence," *Philosophical Forum* 4 (1972–1973): 74–86
31. "Finite things were contingent in themselves but necessary with reference to their causes and ultimately to God, who is the Cause of causes. Thus the natural order retains its integrity and the continuity of its categories – time, space, causalty, the wholeness of human intelligence, and moral sense" (Goodman, *Avicenna*, p. 74).

thought, was the very antithesis of a created one. An eternal world cannot be dependent upon an act of God.[32] In fact, al-Ghazālī claims that, even on philosophical grounds, all the arguments advanced for an eternal world fail.

Later in the twelfth century Averroes [ca. 1126–1198], in *The Incoherence of the Incoherence* [*Tahāfut al-Falāsifah*] defended the Greek philosophical tradition against al-Ghazālī.[33] Averroes argued that eternal creation is not only intelligible, but is "the most appropriate way to characterize the universe."[34] Al-Ghazālī thought that for God to be the cause of the world, that is, for God to be the agent who brings about the existence of the world, such causality required a temporal beginning. In other words, the world cannot be both eternal and the result of God's action, since whatever is the result of an action of another must come into existence after the initiation of the action of the other. Thus, what exists eternally cannot have another, not even a divine other, as its originating source. In reply, Averroes draws a distinction between two different senses of an eternal world: eternal in the sense of being unlimited in duration, and eternal in the sense of being eternally self-sufficient, without a first cause:

> If the world were by itself eternal and existent ... then, indeed, the world would not have an agent at all. But if it is eternal in the sense that it is an eternal [process of] origination and that its origination has neither beginning nor end, then certainly that which conveys the meaning of eternal origination has a

32. *Tahāfut al-Falāsifah*, discussions 1–4. Goodman summarizes al-Ghazālī's central point: "The Philosophers [like Avicenna] wanted to show the world's timeless dependence upon God, but the idea of timelessness demands that of self-sufficiency, and Ibn Sīnā's conception of creation as contingent in itself and necessary with reference to its cause only papers over a contradiction" (Goodman, *Avicenna*, p. 83).

33. For a brief summary of Averroes' philosophical thought, see Deborah L. Black, "Averroës," in *Medieval Philosophers*, ed. Jeremiah Hackett, *Dictionary of Literary Biography* 115 (Detroit: Gale Research, 1992), pp. 68–79. See also *Multiple Averroès: Actes du Colloque International organisé à l'occasion du 850e anniversaire de la naissance d'Averroès, Paris 20–23 septembre, 1976*, ed. Jean Jolivet (Paris: Belles Lettres, 1978); Dominique Urvoy, *Ibn Rushd (Averroes)*, translated by Oliva Stewart (London: Routledge, 1991), and Kogan, *Averroes and the Metaphysics of Causation*.

34. Kogan, *Averroes and the Metaphysics of Causation*, p. 203.

greater right to be called 'creation' than that which conveys the meaning of limited creation. In this way the world is God's creation and the name 'origination' is even more suitable for it than the word 'eternity.' The philosophers only call the world eternal to safeguard themselves against [being identified with those who believe in] the kind of creation which is from something, in time, and after a state of non-existence.[35]

As we have seen, the early Church Fathers who argued so strongly against the Greek notion of the eternity of the world were convinced that that notion was obviously incompatible with the doctrine of creation. Averroes notes that a world which is eternal only in the first sense of eternal, that is, unlimited in duration, would still require an external agent which makes it what it is. Thus, what makes the world eternal – in this first sense of eternal – could be identified with that which causes it to be. On the other hand, a world which is eternal not only in the sense of unlimited duration but also in the sense of being completely self-sufficient would be entirely independent of any external cause. Its eternal existence would be rooted simply in what it is: it would exist necessarily, without cause. Averroes contends that philosophers, such as Aristotle, are committed to the eternity of the world only in the sense of unlimited duration and not in the sense of the world's being wholly self-sufficient. The distinction he draws, thus, is between a world which is eternally existent in itself and a world which is eternally existent by being made so.

Even though Averroes claimed that an eternal, created universe was indeed probable, he rejected the idea of creation out of nothing in its strict sense. He thought that creation consisted in God's eternally converting potentialities into actually existing things. For Averroes, the doctrine of creation out of nothing contradicted the existence of a true natural causality in the universe:

> [al-Ghazālī's] assertion [in defense of creation out of nothing]...
> that life can proceed from the lifeless and knowledge from
> what does not possess knowledge, and that the dignity of the

---

35. Averroes, *Tahāfut al-Tahāfut* 162; trans. Simon Van den Bergh, *The Incoherence of the Incoherence*, 2 vols. (London: Luzac, 1954), 1: 96–97, as quoted (with modifications) by Kogan, ibid., p. 205.

First consists only in its being the principle of the universe, is false. For if life could proceed from the lifeless, then the existent might proceed from the non-existent, and then anything whatever might proceed from anything whatever, and there would be no congruity between causes and effects, either in the genus predicated analogically or in the species.[36]

Earlier in the *Tahāfut* Averroes observes that in a universe without real natural causation, "specific potentialities to act and to be acted upon are reduced to shambles" and causal relations "to mere happenstance."[37] Thus, for Averroes, there could be no science of nature if the universe were created out of nothing. In several long commentaries on various treatises of Aristotle, Averroes rejects Avicenna's theory of emanation and argues that God's connection to the universe ought to be understood in terms of final causality.[38] Averroes is critical of what he considers to be Avicenna's confusion of metaphysics and physics, in particular, the introduction of the argument for the prime mover into metaphysics.[39] Also, in defense of real causality in nature, Averroes is troubled by Avicenna's reliance on the immediate action of immaterial agents (separated forms) in the various changes in the physical world.

Averroes' interpretation of Greek philosophy, in particular his commentaries on the texts of Aristotle,[40] plays an important role in discussions in the thirteenth century concerning creation and the eternity of the world. Also important is the thought of another twelfth century thinker, the Jewish theologian and philosopher, Maimonides [1135–

36. *Tahāfut al-Tahāfut* 452, trans. Van den Bergh 1: 273; also quoted in Kogan, *Averroes*, p. 353.

37. Kogan, *Averroes and the Metaphysics*, p. 218.

38. Particularly in his *Long Commentary on Aristotle's 'Metaphysics'* (ca. 1190); see Black, "Averroës," p. 77.

39. Roger Arnaldez observes that "unlike Avicenna who strives to deduce, at least theoretically, the physical from the metaphysical, Averroes is essentially a philosopher of nature. In a passage of commentary on Book L of the *Metaphysics*, he writes, in express opposition to Avicenna, that unless the metaphysician instantly requested of the physicist that he pass on to him the idea and the reality of movement, he would have no knowledge of it. Physics is therefore fundamental, and metaphysics simply crowns the whole structure of the positive sciences." See Arnaldez, "L'histoire de la pensée grecque vue par les Arabes," *Bulletin de la Société Française de la Philosophie* 72 (1978): 168.

40. Aquinas will refer to Averroes as "the Commentator."

1204].[41] In his monumental *The Guide of the Perplexed*, Maimonides argues that on the basis of reason alone the question of the eternity of the world remains unresolvable. His arguments on this topic, as well as his interpretation of the thought of Aristotle, influenced thirteenth-century Christian thought.

Along with Averroes, Maimonides was critical of the kalam theologians who assign all causal agency to God. Without the necessary nexus between cause and effect, discoverable in the natural order, the world would be unintelligible and a science of nature would be impossible. The kalam theologians, as Maimonides represents them, give no consideration to how things really exist, for this is "merely a custom," and could just as well be otherwise.

> They [the kalam theologians] assert that when a man moves a pen, it is not the man who moves it; for the motion occurring in the pen is an accident created by God in the pen. Similarly the motion of the hand, which we think of as moving the pen, is an accident created by God in the moving hand. Only, God has instituted the habit that the motion of the hand is concomitant with the motion of the pen, without the hand exercising in any respect an influence on, or being causative in regard to, the motion of the pen.[42]

41. For a comparison of Avicenna, Maimonides, and Aquinas, see: David B. Burrell, *Knowing the Unknowable God: Ibn Sīnā, Maimonides, Aquinas* (Notre Dame, IN: University of Notre Dame Press, 1986), *Freedom and Creation in Three Traditions* (Notre Dame, IN: University of Notre Dame Press, 1993), and "Aquinas and Islamic and Jewish Thinkers." Cf. also Roger Arnaldez, *À la croisée des trois monothéismes: Une communauté de pensée au Moyen Âge* (Paris: Albin Michel, 1993). See also: Marvin Fox, *Interpreting Maimonides: Studies in Methodology, Metaphysics, and Moral Philosophy* (Chicago: University of Chicago Press, 1990); *Maimonides and Philosophy*, ed. Shlomo Pines and Yirmiyahu Yovel (Dordrecht: Martinus Nijhoff, 1986); various essays in *Neoplatonism and Jewish Thought*, ed. by Lenn E. Goodman (New York: State University of New York Press, 1992); Alfred Ivry, "Maimonides on Creation," in *Creation and the End of Days: Judaism and Scientific Cosmology*, ed. David Novak and Norbert Samuelson (Lanham, MD: University Press of America, 1986), pp. 185–213; Avital Wohlman, *Thomas d'Aquin et Maïmonide: un dialogue exemplaire* (Paris: Cerf, 1988), and Davidson, *Proofs for Eternity*.

42. Moses Maimonides, *The Guide of the Perplexed* 1.71 and 73; trans. Shlomo Pines (Chicago: University of Chicago Press, 1963), pp. 179 and 202.

He is also critical of their claims to demonstrate that the world is not eternal but has been created out of nothing. Maimonides thinks that whether the universe is eternal or "temporally created" cannot be known by the human intellect with certainty. The most a believer can do is to refute the "proofs of the philosophers bearing on the eternity of the world." Maimonides criticizes the methods of the kalam theologians, who claim first to demonstrate "the temporal creation of the world" out of nothing and then to argue from such a creation to the existence of God. In fact, he suggests that the better method is to prove that God exists, is One, and is incorporeal, on the *assumption* that the universe is eternal.[43]

Maimonides was particularly alert to what he considered to be the dangers of Neoplatonic emanationism in which the doctrine of creation and the eternity of the world are combined in such a way that would deny the free activity of God. As we have seen, an eternal universe is a natural corollary to the view of creation as emanation. Furthermore, Maimonides recognized that the theory of emanation means that it is necessary that creation occur, that reality pour forth spontaneously and immediately from God: a view which denied God's freedom. In fact, he thought that the Aristotelian commitment to an eternal universe embraced a necessity which was incompatible with divine freedom. Against what he considered to be Aristotle's view, Maimonides claims that "all things exist in virtue of a purpose and not of necessity." Maimonides is clear to distinguish his position from the positions he attributes to the Aristotelians and to the kalam theologians:

> My purpose ... is to explain to you, by means of arguments that come close to being a demonstration, that what exists indicates to us of necessity that it exists in virtue of the purpose of One who purposed; and to do this without having to take upon myself what the Mutakallimun have undertaken – to abolish the nature of that which exists and to adopt atomism, the opinion according to which accidents are perpetually being created, [an opinion they adopt in order to maintain their position of divine causation]. ... [44]

43. *Guide* 1.71; trans. Pines, pp. 180–181.
44. *Guide* 2.19; trans. Pines, p. 303. Marvin Fox observes: "It is clear that Maimonides is trying to preserve what he perceives as the best of two worlds. He is not

If in faith we affirm that God is truly a free agent, then we must reject an eternal universe since, according to Maimonides, such a universe denied God's freedom and eliminated purpose. By the beginning of the thirteenth century, discourse about the origin of the world – and in particular about how to understand creation – is already part of a rich intellectual legacy that incorporates the traditions not only of Greek and Hellenistic thought, but also of Muslim, Jewish, and Christian theology.

Creation in the Thirteenth Century

Centuries of theological speculation on the first verse of Genesis had firmly established, well before the thirteenth century, at least four tenets in the Christian doctrine of creation: that God alone created the universe; that He created the universe out of nothing; that He created the universe immediately without any secondary causes; that He created the universe with a temporal beginning. The sustained discussion concerning the doctrine of creation which occurred in the thirteenth century is part of the wider encounter between the heritage of classical antiquity and the doctrines of Christianity: an encounter between claims to truth founded on reason and on faith.

No matter how certain each of these four tenets was, each of them was the object of some contention in the early thirteenth century. The fact that God alone is the Creator of the universe was challenged by the ancient Manichean heresy which had reappeared as Albigensianism and had spread to southern France by the middle of the twelfth century. Like their ancient counterparts, the Albigenses believed that there were two ultimate and equal principles of the universe, one good and one evil. The fact that God creates out of nothing was challenged by the doctrine of pantheism, which was condemned at the Council of Paris (1210) in John Scotus Eriugena's *De divisone naturae*, because of

---

willing to yield to the extreme results of either the Kalam or the Aristotelians. Like the Kalam he wants to preserve the doctrine of creation in time, and like Aristotle he wants to preserve the fixed order of nature in the sublunar world. Against the Kalam, he rejects their atomism and its concomitant denial of the order of nature, and against Aristotle, he rejects the extension of sublunar necessity to the supralunar world and its concomitant denial of a purposive Creator" (*Interpreting Maimonides*, p. 282).

the use made of this work by Amaury of Bène and David of Dinant.[45] The attraction of Neoplatonism, especially in the school of Chartres, seemed to make the Creator too much like the Demiurge in Plato's *Timaeus*. The fact that God creates all things immediately was challenged by the arrival in the Latin West, already by the twelfth century, of works which taught the doctrine of emanationism, works such as the *Liber de causis*.[46] These works would soon be supplemented by those of al-Fārābī and Avicenna so that the Latin West had a thorough exposure to the doctrine that God's creative causality was necessarily mediated through subordinate causes (various levels of "intelligences"). Finally, against the fact that the world had a temporal beginning, came the doctrine, especially from Aristotle, that the world is eternal.

45. In the late twelfth century there was considerable confusion as to what constituted the real Aristotelian corpus. Amaury tried to use Aristotle's *Physics* to explain the nature of God's existing in all things. He had at his immediate disposal Eriugena's *De divisione naturae (Peri physeon)*, in which the Logos and all creation were seen to emanate from God as from the *nihil* "from which all things are made" and "in which all things exist." For him, the *nihil* was like the neo-Platonic non-being which is beyond all being and also something like Aristotle's prime matter from which all things come. David of Dinant began teaching Aristotle's *Physics* in the arts faculty at Paris in the first decade of the 13th century, and he explicitly identified Aristotle's pure potentiality of prime matter with the nothingness of God, which transcends all human understanding. Obviously, if Aristotle teaches that God is prime matter his views are incompatible with Christianity. In 1210 the archbishop of Sens convoked a council of bishops in Paris to discuss the matter. In the decree issued by the council, the body of Amaury was to be exhumed and buried in unconsecrated ground; he was to be excommunicated; the writings of David of Dinant were to be burned; and "the books of Aristotle on natural science or any commentaries on them were not to be read at Paris publicly or privately." See *Chartularium Universitatis Parisiensis*, ed. Heinrich Denifle and Emile Chatelain, 4 vols. (Paris: Delalain, 1889–1897), 1: 70. See Etienne Gilson, *A History of Christian Philosophy in the Middle Ages* (London: Sheed & Ward, 1955), pp. 240–244.

46. The *Liber de causis* [*Book of Causes*] was taken largely from Proclus' *Elements of Philosophy* and presented a Neoplatonic view of emanationism. The work, however, was thought by many in the Middle Ages to have been written by Aristotle. When Aquinas wrote his own commentary on the text (1271–1272), he recognized that the work could not have been written by Aristotle. When Aquinas comments on the *Sentences* of Peter Lombard he still thinks that the *Liber de causis* is authentically Aristotelian. See Aquinas, *Commentary on the Book of Causes*, trans. and annotated by Vincent A. Gualiardo, Charles R. Hess, and Richard C. Taylor (Washington, DC: Catholic University of America Press, 1996).

In the late twelfth and early thirteenth centuries there was considerable disagreement about the position of Aristotle on the eternity of the world. Any attempt to address the issue had not only to confront the authority of Maimonides who denied that Aristotle had claimed to demonstrate that the world is eternal,[47] but also to contend with the state of the Aristotelian corpus, with its spurious and ambiguous texts (e.g., from Aristotle's *Topics*) and the vagaries of translations, as well as the predisposition to read Aristotle in the best light, an *expositio reverentialis*, according to which the philosopher could not be construed as contradicting fundamental Christian doctrine. Roger Bacon, one of the early interpreters of Aristotle, noted that the idea of an eternal world was so obviously absurd that it could not be attributed to Aristotle. How could Aristotle, who denied the possibility of an actual infinity, think that there was an unending number of past days?[48]

Regardless of what early thirteenth-century Christians thought about Aristotle, there was no disagreement that, in fact, the universe is not eternal and that it has been created *ex nihilo* by God. In 1215 the Fourth Lateran Council proclaimed as much, a proclamation which was directed, at least in part, against Albigensianism:

> We firmly believe and simply confess that there is only one true God, ... one origin [*principium*] of all things: Creator of all things, visible and invisible, spiritual and corporeal; who by His own omnipotent power from the beginning of time [*ab initio temporis*] all at once made out of nothing [*de nihilo con-*

---

47. Maimonides distinguishes between Aristotle and Aristotelians. The latter assumed that Aristotle had *demonstrated* the eternity of the universe. On the contrary, according to Maimonides, despite the various arguments Aristotle advances in favor of the eternity of the universe, Aristotle was well aware that he "possesses no demonstration" concerning the eternity of the universe (*Guide* 2.15; trans. Pines, p. 289).

48. Cf. Roger Bacon, *De viciis contractis in studio theologie* (ca. 1290), p. 10; cited by Richard C. Dales, *Medieval Discussions of the Eternity of the World* (Leiden: Brill, 1990), pp. 191–192 n31. The same argument was used by Philoponus: see Luca Bianchi, *L'errore di Aristotele: La polemica contro l'eternità del mondo nel XIII secolo* (Firenze: La Nuova Italia Editrice, 1984), pp. 20–24. See also *The Eternity of the World in the Thought of Thomas Aquinas and His Contemporaries*, ed. J.B.M. Wissink (Leiden: Brill, 1990).

didit] both orders of creation, spiritual and corporeal, that is, the angelic and the earthly. ...[49]

The decree of 1215 is the first formal conciliar statement by the Church that the world had a temporal beginning. The question of the world's temporal finitude occupied the attention of theologians and philosophers throughout the century. In 1277 Etienne Tempier, the Bishop of Paris, issued a list of propositions condemned as heretical, among them the claim that the world is eternal.[50] As Chancellor of the University of Paris, the bishop was well aware of the debates about creation and the eternity of the world which raged throughout Latin Europe in the thirteenth century. The recently translated treatises of Aristotle (and his Muslim commentators) in the natural sciences and metaphysics provided an arsenal of arguments which appeared, at least, to be contrary to the truths of Christianity. In particular, how is one to reconcile the claim, found throughout Aristotle, that the world is eternal with the Christian affirmation of creation, understood as meaning that the world is temporally finite?

Bishop Tempier's condemnations reflect the concern that he and other theologians had concerning heterodox views on the subject of creation being taught in the arts faculty of the university. These condemnations are evidence of the extent and intensity of the debate concerning the relationship between faith and reason. For example, is the knowledge that the world is not eternal exclusively a matter of faith? Surely, if it is true that the world has a beginning of its duration there can be no truly demonstrative argument for its eternity; one truth

---

49. *Enchiridion Symbolorum* §428, ed. Heinric Denzinger (Freiburg: Herder, 1932), p. 199.

50. In 1270 Tempier issued a smaller list of condemned propositions. Articles 83 to 92 of the 1277 list concern propositions which in various ways affirm that the world is eternal. See Roland Hissette, *Enquête sur les 219 articles condamnés à Paris le 7 mars 1277* (Louvain: Publicationes Universitaires, 1977); Luca Bianchi, *Il vescovo e i filosofi: La condanna parigina del 1277 e l'evoluzione dell'Aristotelismo scolastico* (Bergamo: Pierluigi Lubrina, 1990); Kurt Flasch, *Aufklärung im Mittelalter? Die Verurteilung von 1277. Das Dokument des Bischofs von Paris* (Mainz: Dieterich, 1989); John Murdoch, "The Condmenation of 1277, God's Absolute Power, and Physical Thought in the Late Middle Ages," *Viator* 10 (1979): 211–244; and John Wippel, "The Condemnations of 1270 and 1277 at Paris," *Journal of Medieval and Renaissance Studies* 7 (1977): 169–201.

cannot contradict another truth. Since the world has a temporal beginning, can reason demonstrate that this must be so? What can reason demonstrate about the fact of creation itself, as distinct from the question of a temporal beginning of the world? Indeed, can one speak of creation distinct from a temporally finite universe? These are some of the questions which thirteenth-century Christian theologians and philosophers confronted.

From his earliest to his last writings on the subject, Aquinas maintains that it is possible for there to be an eternal, created universe.[51] On the basis of faith Thomas holds that the universe is not eternal. But he thinks that God could have created a universe which is eternal. Although reason affirms the intelligibility of an eternal, created universe, Aquinas thought that reason alone leaves unresolved the question of whether the universe is eternal. The development by Thomas of an understanding of creation *ex nihilo*, and, in particular, his understanding of the possibility of an eternal, created universe, offers one of the best examples of his account of the relationship between faith and reason. In fact, his magisterial treatment of the doctrine of creation is one of the enduring accomplishments of the thirteenth century. It is an accomplishment that sets him apart from his predecessors and his contemporaries.

Contrary to the claims of Averroes, for example, Aquinas thought that a world created *ex nihilo* (whether that world be eternal or temporally finite) was susceptible to scientific understanding. Creation so understood does not destroy the autonomy of that which is created: created beings can and do function as real secondary causes, causes which can be discovered in the natural sciences. Nor does an eternal universe have to mean, as Maimonides, al-Ghazālī, and others argued, a necessary universe, a universe which is not the result of the free creative act of God. An eternal, created universe would have no first moment of its existence, but – as Avicenna had noted – it still would have a cause of its existence.

---

51. John Wippel argues that Aquinas only late in his life stated *explicitly* that an eternal, created universe is possible: see "Did Thomas Aquinas Defend the Possibility of an Eternally Created World? (The *De aeternitate mundi* Revisited)," in *Journal of the History of Philosophy* 29 (1981): 21–37. Even if Wippel is right, however, it does not mean that Aquinas has changed his position on the question.

Albert the Great (*ca.* 1200–1280), Aquinas' own teacher, denied that reason could come to a satisfactory understanding of creation:

It ought to be said that creation is properly a divine work. To us, moreover, it seems to be astounding in that we cannot conclude to it because it is not subject to a demonstration of reason. And so not even the philosophers have known it, unless perchance some [should have known something] from the sayings of the Prophets. But no one ever investigated it through demonstration. Some, to be sure, have found certain probable reasons, but they do not prove [creation] sufficiently.[52]

52. *Super Sententiarum libros* 1.8, *Opera omnia,* ed. Auguste Borgnet, 38 vols. (Paris: Ludovico Vivès, 1890–1899), 27: 22). When Albert in his commentary/paraphrase of the *Liber de causis,* a work of his maturity, states that *esse* is a created thing and that all of the ancients held that *esse* is created *ex nihilo,* his explanation is in terms of formal not material causality. For Albert, here, *esse* is the ultimate formality of a thing (*Liber de causis* 2.1.17, *Opera omnia,* ed. Borgnet 10: 461–463). If one resolves a thing into its ever more universal formalities, along the lines say of a Porphyrian tree, one ultimately resolves to the most universal formality of all, namely, *esse.* Man, for example, can be considered as rational, as animal, as material substance, and finally, the most common formality of all, as being. There is literally nothing [*nihil*] intrinsic to a thing that is prior to the formality of *esse.* Thus *esse* is created *ex nihilo* in the sense that there is nothing prior formally to *esse.* Only *esse* is said to be created; none of the formalties subsequent to *esse* is said to be created. Thus, in man, the formalities of *vivere, sentire,* and *ratiocinari* are not created but merely caused, or informed, for they are not *ex nihilo.* The Christian doctrine of creation, on the other hand, holds that the entire thing – all of what a thing is in any way – is created. In his own *Summa theologiae, sive mirabili scientia Dei* Albert explains that the philosophers take the word "creation" to mean something quite different from what Christians mean: "Creation – understanding: what comes to be from a pure nothing – they [the ancient philosophers] could not know through reason" (1.13.53.1; *Opera omnia,* ed. Borgnet, 31: 544b) .

Steven Snyder argues that, although Albert early in his career thought that creation was not demonstrable, by the time he completed his paraphrase on Aristotle's *Metaphysics* he concluded that there was such a demonstration for the origination of all things out of nothing. Albert, according to Snyder, came to recognize that the making of something after nothing [*faciens aliquid post nihil*] does not require that "after" have any temporal connotation ("Albert the Great: Creation and the Eternity of the World," in *Philosophy and the God of Abraham,* ed. R. James Long (Toronto: Pontifical Institute of Mediaeval Studies, 1991), pp. 191–202). For an alternate view, see Lawrence Dewan, "St. Albert, Creation, and the Philosophers," *Laval théologique et philosophique* 40 (1984): 295–307.

Yet, in the text we have translated, Aquinas claims: "Not only does faith hold that there is creation, but reason also demonstrates it."[53] Central to Aquinas' philosophical explication of creation is his understanding of the real distinction between existence and essence in creatures and their real identity in God. Aquinas' discussion of this theme has been the subject of considerable scholarly reflection in the twentieth century. Etienne Gilson, for example, argued that the inspiration for Aquinas' analysis of creation is to be found in the passage in Exodus in which God reveals Himself as "I am Who am." It is this "metaphysics of Exodus," according to which God claims to be being itself, the unique possessor of being, beyond all temporal conditions, which Gilson finds first in Augustine and then brought to its most sophisticated form in the thought of Aquinas. According to Gilson, the revelation in Exodus "lays down the principle from which henceforth the whole of Christian philosophy will be suspended ... . There is but one God and this God is Being, that is the corner-stone of all Christian philosophy, and it was not Plato, it was not even Aristotle, it was Moses who put it in position."[54]

Gilson claimed that the eternal and necessary world of Greek philosophy was fundamentally different from the created world of Christian revelation. For him, Aristotle's first cause explains why the universe is the way it is, not why it is.

Lawrence Dewan, in a recent article critical of Gilson's interpretation of Aquinas,[55] argues that Gilson's commitment to the importance of Christian philosophy and its unique understanding of *ens inquantum est ens* (being as being) led him to misunderstand several key texts in which Aquinas attributes a doctrine of creation to Aristotle. In Appendix D we have translated a few of the passages from Aquinas in

53. Article Two, solution; see p. 74 below.
54. *The Spirit of Mediaeval Philosophy* (New York: Scribner's, 1940), p. 69.
55. "Thomas Aquinas, Creation, and Two Historians," *Laval théologique et philosophique* 50 (1994): 363–387. Cornelia J. de Vogel has argued, against Gilson, that Greek philosophy did identify God with being – an identification that Christianity appropriated: see "*Ego sum qui sum* et sa signification pour une philosophie chrétienne," *Revue des sciences religeuses* 35 (1961): 337–355. Walter Beierwaltes thinks that Neoplatonic ontology, especially in the thought of Augustine and Boethius, was particularly important in setting the intellectual foundations for the Christian God's being viewed as *ipsum esse subsistens*: see *Platonismus in der Philosophie des Mittelalters* (Darmstadt: Wissenschaftliche Buchgesellschaft, 1969).

which the attribution is clear. Dewan also notes that whereas Gilson emphasizes the contingent character of being a creature, Aquinas refers to the creation of both necessary and contingent beings.[56]

For Aquinas, reason alone can arrive at an understanding of the essential features of the doctrine of creation – of everything, that is, but the temporal beginning of the world. Aquinas also thinks that the causality of Aristotle's unmoved mover is able to be understood – or perhaps expanded to include – the causality of creation. Despite the difficulties that the attribution of an understanding of creation to Aristotle raises for Aristotelian scholars, it reveals the extent to which Aquinas finds a complementarity between reason and faith.[57]

56.   Aquinas distinguishes the necessary from the contingent by noting (following Aristotle) that to be necessary means "cannot be otherwise." In fact, Aquinas generally distinguishes between necessary and contingent beings *in the created order*: "Among the parts of the whole universe, the first distinction to be observed is between the contingent and the necessary. For the highest beings are necessary, incorruptible, and immobile" [*Summa contra Gentiles* 3.94]. For Aquinas there are beings which are absolutely necessary because in them there is no potency to non-being. Material beings, on the other hand, possess a potency with respect to other forms and thus "can be other" than they are. Aquinas often observes that "to be simply necessary is not incompatible with the notion of created being" [*Contra Gentiles* 2.30]. "Things are said to be necessary and contingent according to a potentiality that is in them, and not according to God's potentiality." [*Contra Gentiles* 2.55] God, as necessary being, is necessary *per se*; created necessary beings have a cause of their being, and hence of the fact that they cannot be otherwise. For a useful discussion of contingency and necessity in Aquinas, and how they relate to his notion of creation, see Jan Aertsen, *Nature and Creature: Thomas Aquinas's Way of Thought* (Leiden: Brill, 1988), pp. 236–248. Referring to the last passage cited from the *Summa contra Gentiles*, Aertsen observes that for Aquinas: "Necessity and contingency in things are distinguished not with reference to the first cause, God, but in relation to their next causes, the intrinsic principles of form and matter. Both modes of being do find their ultimate origin in God. For He is the universal cause of being, thus also of the differences of being, the contingent and the necessary. In keeping with the *lex necessitatis vel contingentiae* (*In VI Metaph.*, lec. 3, 1222) set by Him, the causality of finite things is ordered. The creating cause itself transcends this order" (p. 243).

57.   Robert Sokolowski thinks that Aquinas' elaboration of the "metaphysics of *esse* ... does not focus sufficiently on the contrast between such metaphysics and the pagan philosophy of being." For Sokolowski, the doctrine of creation is at the boundary between reason and faith in that it requires a radical distinction between the Creator and creature, a distinction unknown, indeed unknowable, to pagan thought: see *The God of Faith and Reason: Foundations of Christian Theology* (Notre

Aquinas as Bachelor of the *Sentences* of Peter Lombard

By the time the young Thomas Aquinas (b. 1224), a member of the new Order of Preachers, came to Paris in 1245 to live in the Dominican priory of Saint-Jacques and to study with Albert the Great, already a Master in theology, the University of Paris was recognized as a center of theological and philosophical learning.[58] He also arrived at a time when tension was mounting between the secular masters and the members of the mendicant orders. In 1248 Aquinas accompanied Albert to Cologne where the latter was to help to establish a new *studium generale* of the Dominican Order.[59] On Albert's recommendation, Thomas returned to Paris in 1252 to complete the second stage on the road to his becoming Master of theology. At Cologne Thomas had given cursory lectures on the Bible; his teaching at Paris began with lectures on the *Sentences* of Peter Lombard. As *baccalarius Sententiarum* (or *Sententiarius*) Aquinas was only twenty-seven when he arrived in Paris in 1252, and over the next four years as he lectured on the *Sentences* he compiled a commentary known as *Scriptum super libros Sententiarum.*[60] (Although *scriptum* is singular in Latin, we have chosen to translate it as "writings" since we think this is the proper English id-

---

Dame: University of Notre Dame Press, 1982), p. 112. See also, John F.X. Knasas, "Aquinas' Ascription of Creation to Aristotle," *Angelicum* 73 (1996): 487–506

58. When Thomas arrived in Paris to study it was only thirty-five years after the first Dominicans had arrived "to study, preach, and establish a priory": see, James Weisheipl, *Friar Thomas d'Aquino: His Life, Thought and Works,* 2nd ed. with corrigenda and addenda (Washington, DC: Catholic University of America Press, 1983), pp. 53–54. Master was the highest academic rank at the medieval university. For an excellent recent survey of the thought of Albert the Great, see the special issue of the *American Catholic Philosophical Quarterly* 70 (1996), and James Weisheipl, "The Life and Works of St. Albert the Great," in *Albertus Magnus and the Sciences: Commemorative Essays,* ed. Weisheipl (Toronto: Pontifical Institute of Mediaeval Studies, 1980), pp. 13–51.

59. Secular masters were members of the secular clergy, that is, the clergy of a particular diocese; the mendicant masters were members of either the Dominican or Franciscan orders: they are "regular" clergy in that they followed a special rule (including, for example, a vow of poverty). A Dominican *studium generale* was a house of studies for the education, in theology, of members of the order.

60. As *cursor biblicus* Thomas provided students with a rapid, introductory reading (or "run-through") and commentary on the Bible. It is worth noting that although Aquinas became *Sententiarius* at an early age, his predecessors in the role had been in their forties: see Weisheipl, *Friar Thomas d'Aquino,* p. 53.

iom for what Aquinas is doing.) The work is not strictly a commentary but rather writings (*scripta*) or elaborations of the text in the form of questions and discussions of themes which arise from the text. As "bachelor of the *Sentences*," Aquinas read aloud a passage from the text, which he then analyzed. He explained briefly the meaning of the points made and then addressed a question or series of questions arising from the subject of the text.

Peter Lombard (*ca*. 1095–1160) was a twelfth-century scholar and bishop of Paris (1159–1160) who brought together a systematic collection of patristic texts designed to explore the central tenets of the Christian faith. Lombard taught in Paris for more than twenty years and by 1157/58 he completed the final version of his *Sentences*. There were many collections of such "sentences" in the early twelfth century, originating largely from the school of Laon under Anselm and Ralph. In addition to texts from the Church Fathers, Lombard also drew upon biblical texts to assemble a four part-work organized around: (1) the Trinity (essence of the Trinity and the relations among the Three Persons) with some consideration of trinitarian presence in the world and in the life of Christians; (2) God as Creator and creatures (creation in general, the creation and fall of angels, the creation and fall of man, grace, and original and actual sin); (3) the Incarnation of the Word and Christ's work of redemption, to which is annexed a discussion of the virtues and the gifts of the Holy Spirit; (4) the doctrine of the sacraments and a discussion of the last things.[61]

In the preface to his work, Lombard said that his aim was to present sacred doctrine "in a small volume consisting of patristic views (*Patrum sententias*) together with their testimony so that the inquirer would not have to search through numerous tomes, for the synthesized brevity which he seeks is offered here without much labor."[62] Some theologians attacked Lombard and other authors of *sententiae* for

---

61. A modern edition of Peter Lombard's *Sentences* has been edited by Ignatius Brady, *Sententiae in IV Libris distinctae*, 2 vols. (Rome: Collegium S. Bonaventurae, 1971–1981). On the organization of the work see Ignatius Brady, "Pierre Lombard" [1986], in *Dictionnaire de spiritualité*, ed. Marcel Viller et al. 16 vols. (Paris: Beauchesne, 1932–1995), 12: 1604–1612, at col. 1608. The most extensive treatment of Peter Lombard is the recent work of Marcia Colish, *Peter Lombard*, 2 vols. (Leiden and New York: Brill, 1994). For other collections of *Sentences*, see Weisheipl, *Friar Thomas d'Aquino*, pp. 67–68.

62. Quoted in Weisheipl, *Friar Thomas D'Aquino*, p. 68.

preferring scholastic subtleties to the simplicity of the Bible.[63] Nevertheless, by the early thirteenth century Lombard's four books of sentences had become a standard text at the new University of Paris and, as a result, they were the subject of lectures and commentaries.

In many ways Aquinas' *Writings on the Sentences* contain the major themes of his entire intellectual life as theologian and philosopher. James Weisheipl, the noted biographer of Aquinas, observed:

In this earliest work by Thomas, all of his principal conclusions are established: the real distinction between *esse* and essence in creatures and their real identity in God; rejection of the hylomorphic composition of separated substances, or angels; the pure potentiality of first matter; the unicity of substantial form in corporeal creatures; consideration of the agent and possible intellects in man as powers of the individual soul; insistence that matter designated by quantity is the sole principle of natural individuation; insistence that nature is not the 'efficient cause' but only the active principle in the free fall of natural

63. Lombard's work is representative of the development of theology as a science in the twelfth and early thirteenth centuries. M.-D. Chenu provides an excellent account of the distinction between the traditional *collatio* of the monastic schools and the disputations of the new masters. At the heart of the new scholastic methods was the search for causes and reasons, which the defenders of the traditional monastic approach to the Bible rejected. One such defender, Abbot Rupert of Deutz, asked rhetorically why "men would drink out of mere cisterns [of the new scientific learning] when already they had the living fountain of Christ." Chenu also notes a difference between the masters of the twelfth century who, "employing Neoplatonic metaphysics based on Augustine or on pseudo-Dionysius, maintained a more spontaneously religious orientation than their successors, who were equipped with Aristotle as their guide to reason and eventually also their guide to an understanding of nature and of man himself." See Chenu, "The Masters of the Theological 'Science,'" in *Nature, Man, and Society in the Twelfth Century*, trans. Jerome Taylor and Lester K. Little (Chicago: The University of Chicago Press, 1968), pp. 270-309, at pp. 302-303. Recently Marcia Colish has described extensively the development of systematic theology in the twelfth century and the place of scholastic sentence collections as an innovative genre of theological literature: see Colish, *Peter Lombard* 1: 33-90. See also, James Weisheipl, "The Meaning of *Sacra Doctrina* in *Summa theologiae* I, q. 1," *The Thomist* 38 (1974): 49-80; and Marc Aillet, *Lire la Bible avec S. Thomas* (Fribourg: Éditions Universitaires, 1993), pp. 3-40.

bodies; and defense of the possibility of natural motion in a void. In theology also his basic principles stand out clearly: e.g., the hypostatic union of human nature in Christ; transubstantiation of bread and wine into the Body and Blood of Christ; the infinite difference and distinction between what is of nature and what is of grace.[64]

Aquinas will refine, reformulate, and abandon views set forth in this early text, but it stands, nevertheless, as an impressive monument to his skills as theologian and philosopher.

One of the notable features of the *Writings on the Sentences* is the way in which Aquinas divides the material into two categories: the first two books treat of the *exitus* of all things from God, and the second two books, the *reditus* of all things to God – an obvious influence of the Dionysian and Plotinian cycle of emanation and return.[65] Jean-Pierre Torrell observes that there is a deeper theological significance to the structure of *exitus* and *reditus*. That all creatures come from God as first principle finds an analogue in the Trinity: the procession of the Son from the Father. The efficient causality of God, the Creator, can be seen as analogous to the eternal generation of the Son, just as the formal causality of grace, which will permit the return of creatures to God is comparable to the spiration of the Holy Spirit. Thus, one is able to see that the divine mission *ad extra* – creation and redemption – is explained according to the order of the processions of the divine persons *ad intra*.[66] The point is that the structure of Aquinas' *Writings*

64. Weisheipl, *Friar Thomas D'Aquino*, p. 76.

65. Ibid., p. 71. The *Summa theologiae* is organized in the same way: see, for example, R.J. Henle, *Saint Thomas and Platonism: A Study of the 'Plato' and the 'Platonic' Texts in the Writings of Saint Thomas* (The Hague: Martinus Nijhoff, 1956); Cornelio Fabro, "Platonism, Neo-Platonism, and Thomism: Convergencies and Divergencies," *The New Scholasticism* 44 (1970): 69–100; and W.J. Hankey, "Theology as System and as Science: Proclus and Thomas Aquinas," *Dionysius* 6 (1982): 83–93.

66. Jean-Pierre Torrell, *Initiation à saint Thomas d'Aquin, sa personne et son oeuvre* (Paris: Cerf, 1993), pp. 62–64; trans. Robert Royal as *Saint Thomas Aquinas*, vol. 1: *The Person and His Work* (Washington, DC: Catholic University of America Press, 1996), pp. 42–44. See also Francis Ruello, "Saint Thomas et Pierre Lombard. Les relations trinitaires et la structure du commentaire des sentences de saint Thomas d'Aquin," in *Studi Tomistici* 1, s.d. (1974), pp. 176–209; Gilles Emery, "Le Père et l'oeuvre trinitaire de création selon le Commentaire des Sentences de S. Thomas

on the Sentences is chosen not so much for pedagogical purposes, but because it reflects a profound spiritual intuition. The entire universe of creatures, spiritual and material, possesses a dynamic character: analogous to the internal dynamism of the divine persons of the Trinity.[67]

The text we have translated for this volume is in the first part of the second book, the discussion of creation. In the prologue to the entire second book,[68] Aquinas distinguishes the way in which a philosopher considers creatures from the way a theologian does. The philosopher (or broadly speaking the individual who investigates nature with reason alone) examines creatures as natural beings and seeks to discover their causes and properties. The theologian, however, considers creatures "as they come from the first principle and as they are ordered towards their ultimate end, which is God." Philosophical and theological modes of inquiry are complementary; God, after all, is the author of all truth. The first question of the second book concerns the reality and nature of creation, the exposition of which leads to a proper reading (Article Six) of the opening line of Genesis. Although the text before us is part of a larger theological work, Aquinas employs many philosophical arguments in it. In fact, one of the significant accomplishments of Aquinas is the distinction he draws between creation understood philosophically and theologically. Aquinas' understanding of the relationship between reason and faith – and between nature and grace – remains a crowning feature of his work.

---

d'Aquin," in *Ordo sapientiae et amoris: Image et message de saint Thomas d'Aquin à travers les récentes études historiques, herméneutiques et doctrinales,* ed. Carlos Josaphat Pinto de Oliveira (Fribourg, Switzerland: Editions Universitaires Fribourg, 1993), pp. 85–117; Gilfredo Marengo, *Trinità e creazione: Indagine sulla teologia di Tommaso d'Aquino* (Roma: Città Nuova, 1990).

67. Paul Philippe, "Le plan des sentences de Pierre Lombard d'après S. Thomas," *Bulletin thomiste: Notes et communications* 1 (1931–1933): 131*–154*.

68. Appendix E contains a translation of the prologue.

An Analysis of Aquinas'
Writings on the "Sentences" of Peter Lombard,
Book 2, Distinction 1, Question 1

Aquinas discusses creation in an extensive, magisterial way three other times in addition to our text: in *Summa contra Gentiles* 2, cc. 6–38 (1259–1264); in *Quaestiones disputatae de potenia Dei*, q. 3 (1265-1266); and in *Summa theologiae* 1a, qq. 44–46 (1266-1268).[69] Although in a few instances, which will note, Aquinas does change elements of his doctrine in later works, the text from his *Writings on the Sentences* is a particularly good source. Aquinas' exposition of creation here is fuller than that in the *Summa theologiae*, but it does not include so many dialectical arguments, as do his discussions in the *Summa contra Gentiles* and in the *De potentia Dei*. There is not as yet – nor likely to be soon – a critical Latin edition of Aquinas' *Writings on the Sentences*. Despite the difficulties in not having an established text which meets the critical demands of the Leonine Commission, we feel that an English translation of the existing text[70] meets an important need.

Aquinas divides his treatment of creation in this question of the *Writings* into six articles. It is a division of the problem of creation done in typical scholastic fashion: first, the question *an sit*, whether there is creation, i.e., the proofs of creation (Article One); next, the question *quid sit*, the definition of creation (Article Two); finally, the question *de modo*, how does creation proceed (Articles Three, Four, and Five). Article Six is the culmination of the entire *quaestio*: the first five articles elaborate the philosophy and the theology needed for an exposition of the first line of Scripture, which exposition is given in Article Six. Thus, the entire question may be seen as a good example of the use of the scholastic method for the exposition of one line of Scripture: *In principio*

---

69. For a catalogue of Aquinas' works, including dating, see Weisheipl, *Friar Thomas d'Aquino*, pp. 355–405, with corrigenda and addenda at pp. 478-487; and the "Bref catalogue des oeuvres de Saint Thomas," by Gilles Emery, in Torrell, *Initiation à saint Thomas d'Aquin*, pp. 483-525, adapted and translated by Royal for the English version, *Thomas Aquinas*, pp. 330-361.

70. We have used *Scriptum super Libros Sententiarum Petri Lombardi*, ed. P. Mandonnet and M.F. Moos, 4 vols. (Paris: P. Lethielleux, 1929-1947); the relevant text (edited by Mandonnet in 1929) is found in 2: 10-43. We have completed Aquinas' references to Scripture and to Aristotle in the translation itself; we have also completed in the notes all other references Aquinas cites in the text.

creavit Deus caelum et terram. Each article starts with the formulation of a problem to be considered. Aquinas then provides a series of objections to one possible solution. In a section called "on the contrary" [*sed contra*], Aquinas briefly sets out the opposing position, usually supported by references to the Bible, to the Church Fathers, or to short philosophical arguments. In the "solution" Aquinas gives his own position. Finally, he returns to the objections, offering a response to each. It is a mistake to skip over the objections and Aquinas' responses to them. The objections reveal the range of debate on a given topic (as well as Aquinas' desire to be fair to views he opposes), and more often than not Aquinas' responses contain important amplifications of the position found in the solution.

ARTICLE ONE

In the initial objections in Article One, Aquinas explains the twofold nature of the Manichean problem: the fact that there is both good and evil in the world seems to indicate that there must be two ultimate principles of things, one supremely good and the other supremely evil; and the fact that there is contrareity and diversity in the world suggests that there should be a multitude of first principles from which such contrareity and diversity flow. For either reason (or for both) it seems that one must affirm that there is more than one first principle of the world. Against the Manichean position, however, the very nature of a first principle seems to demand that there be only one first principle, for plurality always presupposes unity, and a diversity among first principles can only be accounted for by the fact that the first principles are either composites or not self-sufficient – either of which is repugnant to the nature of a *truly* first principle. (Any composite is necessarily dependent upon something prior, out of which it is composed, and therefore cannot be truly a first principle.)

Aquinas begins his solution to this problem by making a distinction. If by "first" one means, "first in some category or in some order," then it is certainly true that there is more than one first principle of the world: there are as many of these "firsts" as there are orders to be examined. If, however, by "first" one means that which is first without qualification or absolutely [*primum principium simpliciter*], then there can only be one first principle of the world.

Aquinas argues in three ways that there must be only one first principle, and in so doing his arguments amount to proofs that there is a Creator, or proofs for the existence of God. It might, however, be pressing the arguments in the text too far to suppose that just as they are given they constitute Aquinas' philosophical way of coming to know that there is a God. In later works, such as the *Summa contra Gentiles* 1.13, the *Summa theologiae* 1.2.3, and the *Commentary* on Books 7 and 8 of Aristotle's *Physics*, Aquinas will give his philosophical arguments for the existence of God on the basis of a careful analysis of nature, especially, of motion, change, and efficient causality. In Article One we do find the same approach to God, but the approach is much more abbreviated here, because of the context. In this context, Aquinas is arguing against those who recognize some sort of first principle, some sort of transcendent cause or source of the world, but they do not recognize that there is only one, absolutely first cause of all. Aquinas' concern here is not so much to establish that there is an immaterial cause of the universe, for that is already conceded by his opponents,[71] but to show that there can only be one such cause.

First, the very order of the universe, an order obvious to our observation, would be impossible unless all the parts of the universe sought one ultimate principle. The important point for this argument is that the universe as a whole exhibits *one* order: just as the parts of an animal serve one whole order, so the parts of the universe serve one whole order. Aquinas would have thought about the movements of the heavenly bodies which, according to him and to his objectors, are moved, not randomly, but intelligibly and, therefore, by intelligent movers. As these movers are intelligent creatures, they move for the sake of ends; as the end of the universe is one and not many, for the motions of all the heavenly bodies are all coordinated, there must be one end, and not many. In our own day, we reject the cosmology of the heavenly movers, but many physicists would recognize that the precise coordination of the laws of physics shows a degree of order and hence of intelligibility, which affirms an underlying purpose in the universe. Some even go so far as to claim that the laws of nature are

---

71. That there is an immaterial cause of the universe is not, of course, conceded by *some* of Aquinas' opponents, for it is not conceded by the early Greek natural philosophers who were materialists. The materialists, however, were not very sophisticated philosophically and were not Aquinas' primary antagonists.

precisely the laws necessary to produce a universe that can sustain our own lives and the world that we know.[72] This "anthropic principle," as it is sometimes called, is a modern version of what Aquinas recognized: the final causality in the universe as a whole. The specific arguments for an anthropic principle, such as those found in John Leslie[73] and others, may well fail to convince contemporary scientists and philosophers. Our point is simply to note that there is a similarity in approach characteristic of those who argue for an anthropic principle and of Aquinas, and, more generally, that contemporary science does not demand a rejection of the view that there is purpose to be discovered in nature.

In the second way of proving that there is only one first principle, Aquinas argues from the recognition of an order of levels of being. Aquinas thinks that it is obvious that the whole of reality is a hierarchy of perfection in being: lower beings are of a nature that is less perfect than higher beings. This does not refer to individual differences, but to differences of species or of natures. Thus, broadly, a plant is more perfect (in the order of being) than a rock, because a plant has its own principle of life and growth. An animal is more perfect than a plant, because it has not only a principle of growth but also a principle of sensation and motion. Man, next, is superior to animals in possessing rationality and an incorruptible soul. Angels, finally, are more perfect than man in that they are not subject to the mutability and corruptibility of the body and in that their mode of knowing is superior to man's.[74]

72. John Polkinghorne, the distinguished physicist and theologian, puts it this way: "Unless the fundamental physical laws were more or less precisely what they actually are, the universe would have had a very boring and sterile history. In other words, it's only a very special universe, a finely tuned universe, a universe in a trillion, you might say, which is capable of having had the amazingly fruitful history that has turned a ball of energy into a world containing human life" ("So Finely Tuned a Universe of Atoms, Stars, Quanta, and God," *Commonweal* [16 August 1996]: 11–18, at 14).

73. John Leslie, *Universes* (London and New York: Routledge, 1989).

74. The differences among angels themselves can only be accounted for by recognizing the different levels of being, for each angel as an immaterial being is its own unique species. A diversity among immaterial beings can only be the result of differences in the perfection and actuality of the different beings. Such differences must be caused by a first instance of perfection. See *Summa theologiae* 1.50.4.

There cannot be such an order of beings unless there is a highest and a lowest. But it is an order of *beings*, that is, an order from what has the least of being to what has – or, rather, *is* – the most of being.[75] When there is more or less of something in some order, and when there is a first instance of the order, then it is the case that the first instance is the cause of the other instances. The heat in a cabin that is heated by one wood stove, for example, is an order of more and less, in which there is a first instance. The differences in degrees of heat in the cabin, hotter near the stove, cooler farther away, are attributable to the fact that there is a first instance which is the cause of the many secondary instances. Aquinas recognizes the same principle in the order of beings in the world: since there are degrees of being and since there is a first being, the first being must be the cause of the differences in the levels of being among the secondary beings. That is, the first is the cause of being in all other instances of being.

But what does it mean to say that the first being is the cause of being in all of the secondary beings? It means that the first being must truly be able to cause being, and to be able to do so it must not itself stand in need of a cause of being, for if its own being needed to be caused then something else would be the first being. Being (existence) is essential to that which needs no cause of being. Now it is true that for all *creatures* being is not essential, for any creature, any secondary being, can be thought of without thinking that it exists.[76] It is possible,

---

75. As Etienne Gilson has shown, what is distinctive of Aquinas' metaphysics is its focus on *being*, rather than, say, on essence, form, substance, or God. This metaphysical focus is brought out in many places in Gilson's writings, but see, especially, *Being and Some Philosophers*, 2nd ed. (Toronto: Pontifical Institute of Mediaeval Studies, 1952); and *Christian Philosophy*, translated by Armand Maurer (Toronto: Pontifical Institute of Mediaeval Studies, 1993). The point is also evident in the work of Joseph Owens; for an introductory treatment of the problem see his *An Interpretation of Existence* (Milwaukee, WI: Bruce, 1968).

76. As Joseph Owens has shown, however, it is not enough for the metaphysics of Thomas Aquinas to hold that being is accidental for creatures, for if being is considered in another way it is essential to all created things. It is wrong, Owens has argued, to reduce Thomistic metaphysics either to the claim that creaturely existence is accidental or to the claim that creaturely existence is essential. Both claims are true, but neither one is exclusively true. See, "The Accidental and Essential Character of Being," *Mediaeval Studies* 20 (1958): 1–40, rept. in his *St. Thomas Aquinas on the Existence of God: The Collected Papers of Joseph*

therefore, to think of the non-existence of any creature in a way that it is not possible to think that the first being be non-existent. The being and essence, therefore, of the first being are identical.

At the very end of this second way of showing that there is only one first principle, Aquinas adds that the cause of being can only be one since the effect is one. Aquinas is responding to the Manichean affirmation of the plurality of principles. He says that, in a real sense, we are considering the cause of one effect, being, which is the same *by analogy* in all creatures.[77] These words, *by analogy*, are very important, for they indicate that, although "being" means something vastly different for an angel from what it means for a rock, still all things other than God have the same sort of relation to their being. Being is the actuality of an angel, given by God, just as being is the actuality of a rock, given by God. There is a kind of proportionality here between the being of an angel and the being of a rock, for an angel's being is to an angel what a rock's being is to a rock, even though it may be nearly impossible to compare the being of an angel with the being of a rock.

Owens, C.Ss.R, ed. John R. Catan (Albany, NY: State University of New York Press, 1980), pp. 52–96. See our discussion of this problem in the analysis of Article Four, pp. 48–53 below.

77. Even in the study of nature we must use terms analogically: terms such as "motion," "matter," "form," "cause," and the like, when predicated of many different kinds of things, have only a reasonable similarity. In each case of analogical usage there is always some prime analogue, which is best known to us. It is by stretching, expanding, and extending our original definitions and meanings – made possible because of some reasonable similarity – that we form truly analogical concepts. Only by analogy to material things can human beings acquire a glimmer of what immaterial things are like, or, more often, understand what they are not. Thus, we can see why for Aristotle and Aquinas there can be no fully developed metaphysics without a sound physics, because many terms and meanings employed in metaphysics are derived by analogy from what we know much better, namely, the nature of material, sensible things. Similarly, there can be no natural moral law without a well-grounded concept of nature and human nature. All the carefully refined terms and distinctions of natural philosophy are further enlarged analogically in moral philosophy and metaphysics. These refined analogical terms of metaphysics are further expanded throughout the whole of Aquinas' theology to serve to illumine the truths of Christian faith. For a brief, insightful discussion of Aquinas' understanding of analogy, see Wippel, "Metaphysics," in *Cambridge Companion to Aquinas*, ed. Kretzmann and Stump, pp. 85–127, especially, pp. 89–93, and Ralph McInerny, *The Logic of Analogy* (The Hague: Nijhoff, 1961).

The second way, thus, establishes that the order of beings requires a first, and that the first is different from all others in being the unique instance of the identity of essence and existence.

The third way makes a similar point, but in different terms. We know already, from proofs in the *Physics,* that there is some sort of immaterial cause of the world. Suppose, however, that there are several immaterial causes of the world. How will they differ? They will differ in that some will be more actual, have more actuality and less potentiality, than others. One immaterial being will be different from another in that it will have some ability that another will not have; one might, for example, know more than another. This is the crucial point. In order for immaterial beings to differ from one another, one must have some actuality that the other does not. The summit of all such beings will be held by that being that is fully or completely actual, that has all possible actuality in itself and no possibilities unfulfilled or unactualized. In order to be different from this being another being would have to lack some of the actuality of the highest, most actual being. Hence, there can only be one most actual being.

It only remains for Aquinas in this first article to discuss the reasons by which some have been led to think that there must be a plurality of first principles and to respond to the initial objections, which mostly concerned the problem of evil. Thomas's responses constitute an excellent short treatise on the problem of evil. The first deals with the problem of whether evil can exist as a principle; the second with the problem of how evil has a cause, and the third with the problem of whether evil exists for the most part in this world.

ARTICLE TWO

By the end of the first article, Aquinas has only concluded that the first principle "gives being" (*hoc est quod dat esse omnibus*). In the second article, Aquinas' main concern is to explain just what it means for the first principle to give being, that is, his concern is to give a definition of creation *ex nihilo.* The context of the article is the objection, given in a variety of ways, that creation out of nothing is impossible. Fundamentally, each objection contains the assumption, which it is the purpose of this article to refute, that creation is a kind of change. The solution which is at the center of the second article contains another proof of creation, similar to that advanced in Article One, and a long definition of creation out of nothing. The analysis in the solution is Aquinas' finest contribution to the discussion of creation; it contains the essence of his understanding of creation.

Aquinas points out that there are two senses of creation out of nothing, one philosophical, the other theological. The philosophical sense simply means that God, with no material cause, makes all things to exist as entities that are radically different from His own being yet completely dependent upon His causality. This philosophical sense has two essential elements: 1) there is no material cause in creation; 2) the creature is naturally non-being rather than being, which means that the creature is completely dependent, throughout its entire duration, upon the constant causality of the Creator. This is the sense in which creation out of nothing can be proven philosophically (in metaphysics), and this is precisely what Aquinas claims to prove. This is also the sense in which philosophers, such as Avicenna and Aristotle, have proven creation, according to Aquinas.[78] The theological sense of creation denies nothing of the philosophical sense but merely adds to it the notion that the created universe is temporally finite. This theological sense of creation cannot be proven philosophically; it can only be known through revelation.

The creature's dependence upon the cause of its being is precisely the same at the beginning of the creature's duration as it is all throughout its duration. The creature is always of itself literally nothing and

---

78. Later, in his *Commentary on Aristotle's Metaphysics*, Aquinas observes that if "contingent events are traced back further to the highest, divine cause, it will be impossible to find anything that lies outside its [the first cause's] sphere of influence, since its causality extends to all things insofar as they are beings. Hence its causal activity cannot be thwarted as a result of the matter being indisposed, because matter itself and its dispositions do not lie outside the domain of this agent, since He is the agent who gives things their being and not merely moves and changes them" (*In XII Metaph.* 6.3, ed. M.R. Cathala and R.M. Spiazzi [Turin: Marietti, 1950], §1215). On the general subject of Aquinas' attributing a doctrine of creation to Aristotle, see: Steven E. Baldner, "The Doctrine of St. Thomas Aquinas on the Eternity of the World," unpublished MSL Thesis, (Toronto: Pontifical Institute of Mediaeval Studies, 1979); William E. Carroll, "San Tommaso, Aristotele e la creazione," *Annales Theologici* 8 (1994): 365–376; Dewan, "St. Thomas, Aristotle, and Creation," *Dionysius* 15 (1991): 81–90, and "Thomas Aquinas, Creation, and Two Historians," *Laval théologique et philosophique* 50 (1994): 363-387; and Mark Johnson, "Did St. Thomas Attribute a Doctrine of Creation to Aristotle?" *The New Scholasticism* 63 (1989): 129-155.

therefore is in constant need of being created out of nothing. Creation is not merely some distant event; it is the on–going, complete causing of the existence of whatever is. For Aquinas, there is really no difference between creation and what is called conservation; conservation is simply the continuation of creation. In Book 1 of his *Writings on the Sentences*, Aquinas remarks that the relation of a house to its builder is very different from the relation of a creature to the Creator. Once the coming-to-be of the house is complete, the house ceases to have any relation of dependence upon its builder; the builder could die, and the house would continue to stand. But the case is quite otherwise with the creature *qua* creature. The Creator's causality must be continual, and of the same kind, all throughout the creature's existence. All things would fall into non-being, Aquinas says, unless God's omnipotence supported them. "Whence, it is necessary that His [God's] operation, by which He gives being, not be broken off, but be containual." (*In 1 Sent.* 37.1.1). In *De potentia Dei*, Aquinas notes that the operation by which God creates and conserves is the same:

> It ought to be said that God does not produce things into being by one operation and conserve them in being by another. The being [*esse*] of permanent things is not divisible, except accidentally as it is subject to some motion; being, however, exists in an instant. Whence the operation of God does not differ according as it makes the beginning of being and as it makes the continuation of being (5.1, ad 2).

The reason given here for the fact that creation and conservation are the same is not that in God all things are one in His perfect simplicity, but that the effect of God's causality, the being of the creature, is the same effect all throughout the existence of the creature.

It is of particular importance to note that Aquinas does not interpret the expression *ex nihilo*, as so many others did in the thirteenth century, to mean necessarily that God makes the being of the creature to exist temporally after non-being. In the theological, revealed sense of *ex nihilo*, it is true that the created world has a temporal beginning. But there is nothing in the bare meaning of the expression *ex nihilo*, apart from revelation, to indicate that the created world has a temporal beginning. Thus, according to Aquinas, there is nothing in the very meaning of *creatio ex nihilo* that demands that the world have a temporal beginning. He sees no contradiction in the notion of eternal creation out of nothing. In this, Aquinas stands squarely against the position of Bonaventure and of his followers and of most thinkers in the thirteenth century. Bonaventure and Albert the Great, and most of their contemporaries, hold that the very meaning of *creatio ex nihilo* is rationally incompatible with the notion of eternal past duration on the part of the creature.[79] Thinkers such as Bonaventure and Albert were following the analysis of the expression *ex nihilo* that came from Anselm's *Monologion* (c. 8). According to Anselm, if the expression *ex nihilo* is to have any positive meaning, if it is to mean anything more than a mere denial of material causality, then it must indicate a temporal beginning. It was the genius of Aquinas, who acknowledged a considerable to debt to Avicenna on this point, to see that the positive meaning of *ex nihilo* is that the creature is of itself really nothing – its non-being is naturally prior to its being – and that, therefore, the creature is completely dependent upon the Creator for its being. Near the end of his career, in *De aeternitate mundi*, Aquinas will take up, in his most sophisticated treatise on the subject, the intelligibility of an eternal, created universe. There he will write: "to say that something has been made by God and that it has always existed, is not logically inconsistent."[80] We have included a translation of this brief but important treatise in Appendix B.

In addition to the definition of creation given in the solution in Article Two, Aquinas makes clear two points about creation in his responses to the initial objections. First, creation is not any kind of change (*mutatio*). There is no becoming (*fieri*) that precedes the being of the creature; no passive potency precedes the making of the creature.

79. Bonaventure, *Commentaria in IV libros sententiarum* 2.1.1.1.3; Albert the Great, *In 2 Sent.* 1.A.3, ad 1.

80. For an excellent discussion of this text, see Wippel, "Did Thomas Aquinas Defend the Possibility of an Eternally Created World?"; and James Weisheipl, "The Date and Context of Aquinas' *De aeternitate mundi*," in *Graceful Reason: Essays in Ancient and Medieval Philosophy Presented to Joseph Owens*, ed. Lloyd Gerson (Toronto: Pontifical Institute of Mediaeval Studies, 1983), pp. 239–271. See Appendix B for the full text of *De aeternitate mundi*, pp. 114–122 below.

Other thinkers, most notably Bonaventure,[81] will hold that creation is a kind of change, not because they think that there is some becoming or some passive potency in creation, but because they think that creation must mean a temporal beginning. They take the "before" and "after" of creation to be sufficient to indicate a kind of change. Aquinas, on the other hand, resolutely refuses to call creation a change, for he recognizes that a change must always have a material cause or a passive potency of some kind.

Second, although creation is not in the category of change, it can be placed in a category, the category of relation. It is a peculiar type of relation, however, for although the creature is really related to the Creator, the Creator is not really related to the creature. The non-mutual character of creation is essential because God possesses no accidents. If God were really related to the creature, God would undergo an accidental change at the temporal beginning of creation. If x and y are really related to each other, then changes in one necessarily involve changes in the other. Aquinas observes in many places that God is absolutely immutable.[82] Although it is correct to call creation a

81. Bonaventure, *In Sent.* 2.1.1.3.1. See Steven Baldner, "St. Bonaventure on the Temporal Beginning of the World," *The New Scholasticism* 63 (1989): 206–228.

82. "God, who moves all things, must Himself be [un]movable. If He, being the first mover, were Himself moved, He would have to be moved either by Himself or by another. He cannot be moved by another, for then there would have to be some mover prior to Him, which is against the very idea of a first mover. If He is moved by Himself, this can be conceived in two ways: either that He is a mover and moved according to the same respect or that He is a mover according to one aspect of Him and is moved according to another aspect. The first of these alternatives is ruled out. For everything that is moved is, to that extent, in potency, and whatever moves [i.e., changes] is in act. Therefore if God is both mover and moved according to the same respect, He has to be in potency and in act according to the same respect, which is impossible. The second alternative is likewise out of the question. If one part were moving [i.e., causing motion] and another were [being] moved, there would be no first mover himself as such, but only by reason of the part of him which moves [i.e., causes motion] .... Accordingly the first mover must be altogether [un]movable." See *Compendium theologiae* 4, ed. Raimondo A. Verardo, in *Opuscula theologica* (Turin: Marietti, 1954), 1: 14 (§5); trans. Cyril Vollert (St. Louis: B. Herder, 1947), pp. 9–10; see also *Summa theologiae* 1.9.1. For a thorough discussion of God's immutability, see Michael J. Dodds, *The Unchanging God of Love: A Study of the Teaching of St. Thomas Aquinas on Divine Immutability in View of Certain Contemporary Criticism of This Doctrine* (Fribourg: Editions Universitaires, 1986).

relation, we must not forget that the foundation of the relation is God's efficient causality [i.e., His *agere*]. We must also remember that the kind of efficient causality exercised in creation does not involve working with a prior subject.

Elsewhere Aquinas explains that the relation of a knower to the thing known is like the relation of a creature to its Creator; i.e., the relation is non-mutual (*Summa theologiae* 1.13.7). The knower is really related to, and really dependent (for knowledge) upon the knowable thing, but the knowable thing is not in any way affected by the knower. The knowable thing may have a relation of reason (*relatio rationis*) to the knower, but it is not really related to the knower. Similarly, God is not really related to the creature, i.e., He does not depend upon the creature in any way, nor is He affected by the creature, but the creature is completely and constantly dependent upon the Creator. In the creature, the real relation to the Creator has two elements: it is *ad aliud*, i.e., dependent upon God, and it is an attribute inhering in the creature as in a subject. The fact that creation is a real relation in the creature, therefore, indicates both that creation is prior to the creature and that creation is posterior to the creature. In one sense, creation is prior to the creature, for the creature's relation *ad aliud* is a relation of complete dependence upon the Creator, and such dependence is absolutely prior to everything else in the creature. In another sense, creation is posterior to the creature, for creation inheres in the creature like an essential attribute.[83] Creation in the creature, i.e., creation in the passive sense, is both the activity that the creature is constantly receiving in order to exist and the result of that activity, which forms part of the essential make-up of the creature.

ARTICLE THREE

In Article Three, Aquinas takes up the problem of emanationism. Specifically, as he puts it, the problem is whether God can communicate the power of creating to creatures. In other words, can God use creatures as instruments in creation? This article reveals something of Aquinas' personal intellectual history, for later in his life he rejects the position he adopts here. In this article, and only a little latter in his

---

83. For a good discussion of this general topic, see Frederick D. Wilhelmsen, "Creation as a Relation in Saint Thomas Aquinas," *Modern Schoolman* 56 (1979): 107–133.

Quaestiones disputate de veritate (1256–1257), Aquinas allows that it is philosophically possible for God to use some creatures as intermediaries or instruments in the creation of other creatures. Thus, in these two early works, Aquinas grants that the doctrine of emanationism is philosophically plausible, although contrary to the faith, which teaches that God created all things immediately.

Soon after he completed the *De veritate*, Aquinas changed his mind on this question. In the *Summa contra Gentiles* (1259–1264), the *De potentia Dei* (1265–1266), the *prima pars* of the *Summa theologiae* (1266–1268), and the *Quodlibetum tertium* (1270),[84] he argues that it is philosophically impossible for God to communicate in any way the power of creating to creatures. First, the work of creation is a work that requires infinite power; since all creatures are, by nature, finite, they cannot receive, even instrumentally, the infinite creative power (*De potentia Dei* 3.4 sol.). Second, an instrument is only able to cause an effect (instrumentally) that is commensurate with its own form (*Summa theologiae* 1.45.5 sol.) Thus, for example, a saw can cut wood because the action of cutting is commensurate with the properties of the form of the saw. Having sharp, metal teeth belongs to the very essence of a saw; a saw can therefore produce (instrumentally) an effect, the cutting of wood, that is commensurate with its own essence. But since being does not belong essentially to any creature, no creature can be the instrument of the giving of being.

Although Aquinas says clearly, from the *Summa contra Gentiles* on, that no creature can serve as an instrument of creation, he does speak at times as though creatures can be instrumental causes in the conservation of being (*Summa theologiae* 1.104.2). But it is clear that Aquinas means only that secondary causes, such as the heavenly bodies, produce motions that result in conditions that are favorable to creatures on the earth below. When Aquinas speaks of heavenly bodies as conservers of earthly beings, he is careful to point out that the causality of heavenly bodies can never extend beyond motion to the very being of things (*De potentia Dei* 5.1 ad 7). Insofar as one creature is the cause of the well-being of another creature, we may say that the one is the conserver of the other, but one creature can never give being itself to another.

84. *Summa contra Gentiles* 2.20–21; *De potentia Dei* 3.4; *Summa theologiae* 1.45.5 (see below, Appendix A); *Quodlibetum tertium* 3.1.

ARTICLE FOUR

In the fourth article, Aquinas corrects an imbalance that may be present in the reader's understanding of creation. In the first three articles, Aquinas spoke about the being of the creature as though it were something quite accidental to the creature, something that must be entirely caused by God. Of its own nature – that is, left completely to itself – the creature is non-being rather than being, and it must be caused by God continuously lest it return to the non-being which it properly is. It is true to say that the creature is literally nothing without the creative causality of God.

Nevertheless, we must remember that the being of creatures, far from being an accident, is the ultimate perfection or actuality of the creature (*In 1 Sent.* 8.1.3). Most profoundly, in the depths of any creature is its being; a creature is nothing so much as its own being. The creature, thus, far from being an insubstantial, quasi-nothing, is a real something, existing on its own. In giving being to the creature, God does not merely make the creature to be an extension of Himself; rather He gives the creature an inherent stability in being, i.e., a tendency to exist. God gives being in such a way that the tendency of the given being is not to lapse into non-being but precisely to remain in being. God so constitutes the being of creatures that they tend to exist and not to fall into nothingness.[85]

On this point it is helpful to compare the doctrine of St. Bonaventure who, like Aquinas, does not hold that created beings have a tendency to non-existence, but who, unlike Aquinas, thinks that since creatures are *temporal* they need a maintenance in being, called conservation, that is different from their being created in the first place. It is true for both Aquinas and Bonaventure that creatures will cease to exist if God should cease to cause their existence. For Aquinas, however, God gives being, and no other act is required in order to keep creatures in existence. For Bonaventure, on the other hand, God must perform two different acts: He gives being initially and, since the creature cannot naturally maintain its own existence, He conserves the

---

85. "The natures of creatures manifest that no creatures are degenerating into nothing, either because they are immaterial beings, in which there is no potency to non-being, or because they are material beings, and these remain in existence, at least in their matter, which is incorruptible" (*Summa theologiae* 1.2.104.4, sol). See also *De potentia Dei* 5.4.

creature in existence. In other words, according to Bonaventure, if we look at the natural principles of a creature, form and matter, the creature is not mutable into absolute non-being. If, however, we look at the fact that creatures are made out of nothing, we find an inherent emptiness (*vanitas*), instability (*instabilitas*), and mutability (*vertibilitas*). Hence, by nature creatures are mutable into non-being, but by God's grace they are conserved in being.[86]

An illustration of the fact that in Aquinas' doctrine being belongs really to the creature can be found in *De potentia Dei*, where he asks whether God can return the creature to nothing. When Aquinas answers this question he rejects the view of Avicenna, who had argued that the essence of the creature is of itself a pure possibility toward either being or non-being. Aquinas agrees with Averroes in thinking that some creatures, such as immaterial substances and heavenly bodies, have an inherent necessity for existing, for there is in them no possibility for corruption. However, he carries Averroes' point further, arguing that no creature, whether material or immaterial, has any sort of potency for non-being: "... in the whole of created nature, there is no potency through which it is possible for something to tend into nothing" (*De potentia Dei* 5.3 sol.). It is true that material bodies tend to corrupt, but matter itself, prime matter, is incorruptible. The whole of the universe, considered in itself, has its own being and tends to continue in being. Of itself, it has no potency, or tendency, to non-being. However true it may be to say that the creature would be absolutely nothing without the creative causality of God, still, the creature really has its very own being.

Since creatures do have their own being, they are able to be true, autonomous causes. The problem for Article Four is to explain how it is that, although God is the immediate cause of all being, creatures are still true causes of effects. Aquinas' explanation is that creatures are the true causes of whatever comes to be either through motion or generation and that God is the cause of the being of all things, even of that which is produced through motion or generation. God is the constant cause of all being; creatures cause, as it were, only the determinations of being. The creature causes *this* form to be in *this* matter, by bringing the form into actuality from the potency of matter, but God causes the matter to be and thus gives it a potency to form. Creatures, thus, are

---

86. Bonaventure, *In 2 Sent.* 37.1.2 sol.; *In 1 Sent.* 8, 1.2.2 sol, and ad 7–8.

the true causes of most[87] substantial and accidental changes in that they produce the new form, but as to the production of being, God is always the only cause.

Later, in *De potentia Dei* 3.8, Aquinas investigates in greater detail the relationship between creation and "the work of nature." The issue concerns the general problem of how one substance can become another substance and how anything can cause this to happen. Where does the form of the new substance[88] come from? Either the new form always existed, in which case it does not come into being; or it never existed, in which case it cannot come into being. Aquinas describes two erroneous accounts of how new things come to be. According to one view, forms pre-exist in matter; thus generation is but the extraction of one thing from another. The forms of new things are actually present in matter, but hidden, and natural agents produce new things only in the sense that they serve to reveal what is already there. Aquinas thinks that such a view suffers from an "ignorance of matter," a failure to distinguish between potency and act. The forms of things which are produced by nature exist in matter, but only potentially, not actually. Such a distinction between potency and act is essential for making sense of real generation, real novelty, in the world.

Others thought that forms cannot proceed from matter because forms are immaterial realities, and matter is not part of form. Thus, the forms of new things must, quite literally, come from nothing. Natural agents lack the power to produce forms from nothing, and thus a supernatural agent is necessary for the generation of new forms. Real becoming in the world is reduced to an extrinsic *dator formarum* (giver of forms). This is the view of Avicenna, for whom natural forms flow from the lowest of the spiritual substances. Natural agents only prepare matter for the reception of forms; the forms come to be *per viam creationis*,[89] and creation is always mingled with the activity of

---

87. Aquinas points out that creatures cannot be the causes of angels or human souls or heavenly bodies (the latter were not, according to medieval cosmology, subject to contrareity), nor of temporally first members of every species (since no prior members of the species were present to generate these first members).

88. Aquinas accepts Aristotle's understanding of change, in the categories of both substance and accident, which refers to the loss and acquisition of form (substantial and/or accidental).

89. The *dator formarum* is also the "agent intellect" by which the human mind knows all reality. This agent intellect is immaterial and separated from matter, and

natural agents. Aquinas claims that this view arose because of an "ignorance of forms:" the view that the form of a thing is a subsistent entity [a *quod est*]. Aquinas was always alert to avoid the the reification of form or matter; they are principles of things, not things in themselves. Form, for Aquinas, is that whereby a thing is [a *quo est*]. Those things which come to be are composites of form and matter; it is not, strictly, the form which comes to be; it is the *substance*, which has a certain form, which comes to be, subsists, and whose coming-into-being must be explained.

For Aquinas, following Aristotle, forms pre-exist in the potency of matter and they are brought into actuality by natural agents. New forms are not generated by nature out of nothing; they are educed from the potency of matter. Becoming involves natural agency; it is not "mingled" with creation, even though becoming presupposes creation.[90] For Avicenna, the natural agency of fire is sufficient to dispose water to become warmer and warmer, but at the precise moment when the water is sufficiently hot, the *dator formarum* infuses into the water the new form of air to replace the form of water, thus producing a substantial change. For Aquinas, fire is sufficient in itself not only to dispose water to its boiling point (an accidental change), but even to cause water to become air.

The natural sciences seek to discover real causes in the world. In Article Four Aquinas has shown that a doctrine of creation *ex nihilo*, which affirms the radical dependence of all being upon God as its cause, is fully compatible with the discovery of causes in nature. God's omnipotence does not challenge the possibility of real causality for creatures, including that particular causality, free will, which is characteristic of angels and men. The relationship between divine action and the world – both with respect to the natural sciences and human

---

therefore one for all mankind. The individual human mind, although capable of knowing reality, of itself has no form or concept of anything; the new form or concept is infused in the mind by the agent intellect when the mind is disposed toward it. As Weisheipl observes, "It was Avicenna's basic inability to explain how the potential can become actual that made him postulate an extrinsic *dator formarum* to explain the works of nature" ("Aristotle's Concept of Nature: Avicenna and Aquinas," in *Approaches to Nature in the Middle Ages*, ed. Lawrence D. Roberts [Binghamton, NY: State University of New York Press, 1982], pp. 137–160, at p. 150). See also *Summa contra Gentiles* 3.69.

90. See Aertsen, *Nature and Creature*, pp. 319ff.

freedom – continues to be a topic of extended commentary and debate.[91] Some views refer to a divine withdrawal from the world so as to leave room (a metaphysical space) for the action of creatures. Thus, God is said to allow or to permit human freedom. Other views embrace a process theology which denies God's immutability and His omnipotence (as well as His knowledge of the future) so that God is said to be evolving or changing along with the universe and everything in it. For Aquinas, such views fail to do justice either to God or to creation. Creatures are and are what they are (including those which are free) precisely because God is present to them as cause. Were God to withdraw, all that exists would cease to be. Real causality in nature – that which Averroes and Maimonides recognized must be protected against the views of certain of the kalam theologians – is not challenged by divine omnipotence or divine omniscience. Creaturely freedom and the integrity of nature, in general, are guaranteed by God's creative causality, i.e., by God's intimate presence in all that He creates. As Simon Tugwell aptly puts it: "The fact that things exist and act in their own right is the most telling indication that God is existing and acting in them."[92]

91. See *Chaos and Complexity: Scientific Perspectives on Divine Action*, ed. Robert John Russell, Nancey Murphy, and Arthur R. Peacocke (Vatican City: Vatican Observatory Publications, 1995).

92. Simon Tugwell, *Albert and Aquinas: Selected Writings* (New York: The Paulist Press, 1988), p. 213. See also *Summa theologiae* 1.105.5 sol.: "Some have understood God to work in every agent in such a way that no created power has any effect in things, but that God alone is the ultimate cause of everything wrought; for instance, that it is not fire that gives heat, but God in the fire, and so forth. But this is impossible. First, because the order of cause and effect would be taken away from created things, and this would imply lack of power in the Creator, for it is due to the power of the cause, that it bestows active power on its effect. Secondly, because the active powers, which are seen to exist in things, would be bestowed on things to no purpose, if these wrought nothing through them. Indeed, all things created would seem, in a way, to be purposeless, if they lacked an operation proper to them, since the purpose of everything is its operation ... . We must therefore understand that God works in things in such a manner that things have their proper operation ... . Thus then does God work in every worker, according to these three things. First as an end. For since every operation is for the sake of some good, real or apparent; and nothing is good either really or apparently, except in as far as it participates in a likeness to the supreme good, which is God; it follows that God Himself is the cause of every operation as its end. Again it is to be observed that where there are several agents in order, the second always acts in virtue of the first,

For Aquinas, God is at work in every operation of nature, but the autonomy of nature is not an indication of some reduction in God's power or activity; rather, it is an indication of His goodness. To ascribe to God (as first cause) *all* causal agency "eliminates the order of the universe, which is woven together through the order and connection of causes. For the first cause lends from the eminence of its goodness not only to other things that they are, but also that they are causes."[93]

ARTICLE FIVE

In this article, Aquinas takes up the problem of the temporal beginning of the world, and his solution is unique in the thirteenth century.[94] As we noted above, Aquinas held that it would have been possible for the created world to be eternal but that *de facto*, as we know from revelation, the world had a temporal beginning. Others, including Bonaventure,[95] did not see anything contradictory in the idea of mere

---

for the first agent moves the second to act. And thus all agents act in virtue of God Himself; and therefore He is the cause of action in every agent. Thirdly, we must observe that God not only moves things to operate, as it were applying their forms and powers to operation, just as the workman applies the axe to cut, who nevertheless at times does not give the axe its form; but He also gives created agents their forms and preserves them in being. Therefore He is the cause of action not only by giving the form which is the principle of action ...; but also as preserving the forms and powers of things ... . Since the form of the thing is within the thing, since [form] is of more importance as it is prior and more universal, and since God is properly the cause in all things of universal being, which is the most intimate reality in things, it follows that God operates intimately in all things."

93. *De veritate* 11.1; see also *Summa theologiae* 1.22.3, 23.8.2. "Creation is not mingled in the works of nature but is presupposed for the operation of nature" (*Summa theologiae* 1.45.8).

94. See Dales, *Medieval Discussions of the Eternity of the World; The Eternity of the World in the Thought of Thomas Aquinas*, ed. Wissink; Cyril Vollert's introduction to his translation of Aquinas, *De aeternitate mundi, On the Eternity of the World* (Milwaukee, Wisconsin: Marquette University Press, 1964); Bianchi, *L'errore di Aristotele*; Davidson, *Proofs for Eternity*; Sorabji, *Time, Creation, and the Continuum*.

95. Bonaventure did not find it self-contradictory to suppose that something should exist eternally in past time, nor even to suppose that something should be eternally caused in the past. What Bonaventure did find to be self-contradictory was to suppose both the eternal past duration of creatures and their having been created out of nothing (*In 2 Sent.* 1.1.1.2); see Baldner, "Bonaventure on the Temporal Beginning of the World."

eternal past duration, but Aquinas was alone in recognizing that "being created" is fully compatible with "eternal past duration."

As we have already seen, Aquinas recognized the possibility of an eternally created world because he saw that there was nothing in the concept of "being created out of nothing" that indicates the necessity of a temporal beginning. Since there is nothing at all in the meaning of *creatio ex nihilo* to indicate a temporal beginning, because the act of creation does not take any time (it is not like a change that takes place in matter), and since actual causes are always simultaneous with their effects, it would not be unreasonable to say that the created world had eternal duration.[96] Aquinas was able to distinguish between the question of the ultimate origin of the world and whether the world had a temporal beginning. As we saw in Article Two, Aquinas thinks that the philosopher can show that the world has an origin – in that it is dependent upon God as Creator – but the philosopher cannot show that the world has a beginning of its duration.[97]

In defending his own position, Aquinas responds to two extreme positions: that the world is *necessarily* eternal and that the world *necessarily* had a temporal beginning. In this article, Aquinas summarizes the arguments for and against each position. Those arguments for the eternity of the world Aquinas divides into four groups.

1 All generation and corruption presuppose a material substrate. Matter itself, therefore, or prime matter, is ungenerable and incorruptible. Matter, thus, must be eternal. Matter, however, cannot exist apart from form – that is, apart from being informed or determined as some particular thing – so matter and form together must be eternal. Aquinas responds that, although it is true that matter is ungenerable and incorruptible, it does not follow that it always existed, for its primal coming-to-be was not through generation but through creation out of nothing. The error underlying this sort of argument is to think

---

96. Actual, as distinct from potential, causes are always simultaneous with their effects. David Hume, for example, while asleep, is only the potential cause of *The Enquiry Concerning Human Understanding*, but when sitting at his desk and writing the text, he is the actual cause. See Aquinas, *In II Post. anal.* 12.10.2; and William A. Wallace, "Aquinas on the Temporal Relation Between Cause and Effect," *Review of Metaphysics* 27 (1973–1974): 569–584.

97. See also *De potentia Dei* 3.14: "De ratione vero creationis est habere principium originis, non autem durationis; nisi accipiendo creationem ut accipit fides."

that what is true for all natural, physical change must also be true for the act of creation.

2 It is the nature of time to be a flowing reality, always joining the past to the future. If there were a beginning of time, then there would be a time, namely, the very beginning of time, when time did not join the past to the future. Thus, an impossibility would result: there would be a time when time was not really time. Aquinas responds that such an argument is circular, for it defines time in such a way as to preclude the very possibility of what is in question, namely, a temporal beginning, and then it concludes that time could not have a beginning. It is true that, once time has begun, time will always join the past to the future, but it is not true that there must always have been time.

One objection to the intelligibility of a temporal beginning of creation is that it involves the notion of a time before time. In the *Summa contra Gentiles* [2.36.7], Aquinas describes the sense of "before" and "after" involved in speaking about the world's coming-into-existence after it did not exist

> ... the *before* we speak of as preceding time implies nothing temporal in reality, but only in our imagination. Indeed, when we say that time exists *after* not existing, we mean that there was no time at all prior to this designated now; even so, when we declare that *above* the heavens there is nothing, we are not implying the existence of a place outside the heavens which can be said to be *above* in relation to it, but that there is no place at all above it. In either case, the imagination can add a certain dimension to the already existing thing; and just as there is no reason for attributing infinite quantity to a body, as is said in *Physics* III [206b20], so neither does it justify the supposition that time is eternal

3 All motion that takes place can only take place because some prior motion has taken place, either in the mover or in the thing moved. Therefore, all motion must always have been preceded by some motion, and there can be no new motion without a previous motion. Since motion must always be preceded by motion, motion must be eternal. If motion is eternal, that which is moved must be eternal. Therefore, some movable thing has existed eternally. Aquinas

responds that creation is not a change and does not involve any sort of motion. If one wishes to call creation a change, however, it is a change that is preceded not by a change in the mover but only in the movable thing. But since the "movable thing" in the case of creation is really non-being, there cannot be any motion or change of any kind prior to creation. The arguments for the eternity of the world, based on an analysis of time and motion, have their source in Aristotle's *Physics*. In Appendix C we have provided excerpts from Aquinas' *Commentary* on the *Physics*, in which he examines and rejects the demonstrative character of these arguments. In Article Five, Aquinas, following Maimonides, claims that Aristotle himself never thought that there was a demonstration for the eternity of the world; there were only probable arguments. By the time (late 1260's) that Aquinas examines in detail Aristotle's *Physics* he comes, perhaps reluctantly, to the conclusion that Aristotle does claim that he demonstrates that the world is eternal. But even here, as the texts in Appendix D show, Aquinas thinks that Aristotle holds that the world is created

4 If the first cause of the world, either the Creator or the first mover, causes the world to begin in some way, either in being or in motion, it would imply that the first cause underwent a change. There would have to be a "time" when the first cause was not causing the world, and then a "time" later when the first cause was causing the world. For the first cause to go from non-causing to causing would imply that the first cause went from potency to act, i.e., that it underwent a change. The first cause, however, is entirely immutable and could not have undergone a change. The first cause, therefore, causes the world eternally. Aquinas responds by distinguishing among different kinds of efficient causes. An efficient cause that acts necessarily, according to its nature, is determined to its action by the principles of its nature. If it produces something new, it must undergo a change. An efficient cause that acts through will can be one of two kinds: either it acts through an action that is not the very essence of the agent itself, and in such an agent, producing a new effect always implies a change in the agent; or it acts through an action that is its very own essence, and in such an agent (God), producing a new effect does not imply a change in the agent. Since God's willing is His action (*suum velle est sua actio*), God can and does eternally will that certain things have a beginning in time, and He does not have to perform any additional action, other than His eternal willing, to bring about the effect that He has willed. The implication of God's perfect simplicity is that once He has willed to do something He has already done it; if God has willed from all eternity that an effect begin to be at some time, God has *ipso facto* already caused from all eternity the effect to begin to be at its appointed time. God can, thus, without changing Himself at all, will eternally that a new effect, such as the beginning of the world, begin to be.[98]

Although these four arguments presented a radical challenge to the truth as understood by the Church, it was not difficult for Aquinas to respond to them by showing that none of them is demonstrably true. Aquinas, the theologian, also finds that the various arguments which purport to prove what he believes to be true (viz., that world has a temporal beginning) lack probative force. Even though the conclusion each of these arguments reaches is, according to Aquinas, true, he does not think it wise to defend the truths of faith with faulty reasoning. Aquinas analyzes five different sets of arguments which conclude that the world *must* have a temporal beginning.

I To be created is to be made out of nothing. To be made out of nothing is to have being temporally after non-being. Therefore, if the world is created, it cannot be eternal. We have already seen Aquinas' response to this type of argument. To be created out of nothing does not necessarily mean to have being temporally after non-being. Being created out of nothing means having non-being prior to being, but such priority does not imply a temporal priority; it is simply a priority of nature. A priority of nature means that the creature is of itself (i.e., by nature) nothing; in other words, it means that the creature is completely dependent upon the Creator.

II All sound natural philosophers agree that an actual infinite is impossible. If the world is eternal, however, we would have to conclude that there has been an infinite number of past days. It is clear

---

98. This response shows that, for Aquinas, just as the existence of God can be proven, so also can the freedom of God's action. Since God is proven to be subsistent being, we know that there is no difference among God's willing, His nature, and His actions. Furthermore, since we know that being is the perfection of all perfections, the ultimate instance of being must be the instance of ultimate perfection. Since freedom is a perfection, we know that God must be perfectly free. The fact that God's freedom is demonstrable indicates that the position of the emanationists, namely, that God causes necessarily, is demonstrably false.

that there cannot have been an infinite number of past days because, on the one hand, it will have been impossible to have reached the present day, by starting from a day infinitely distant in the past, for one cannot traverse an infinite series, and, on the other hand, no more past days could be added to those already past, for the infinite does not admit of addition. As Aquinas points out, the fundamental mistake of such an objection is the failure to distinguish between things that are successive and things that exist in a complete actuality, *totum simul*. A material thing that is a complete actuality, like a mountain, cannot be infinite, because it has all of its actuality at once (*totum simul*). If a mountain were infinite, an actually infinite amount of matter would be required – which is an impossibility. But for time to be infinite does not mean that anything must be actually infinite. What is actual of time is only the present moment. "There is nothing of time but the present moment," as Aquinas will say in the *Summa*. Time never exists in actuality as a whole (*totum simul*); rather, time is successive and hence has potentiality mixed with act (*Summa theologiae* 1.46.3 ad 3; 1.7.3 ad 4). Thus, by its very nature, time can never be actually infinite. Time is not fully an actual thing, and therefore cannot be an actually infinite thing. Hence, to speak, as the objection does, about "an infinite number of past days" is to reify what does not actually exist. Aquinas' response, therefore, to the objection that if the world is eternal no new days could be added to the already actually infinite past, is clear. If the world is eternal, the past would not constitute an actual infinity, and therefore it would always be possible to add more days.

To the objection that it would be impossible to traverse the series between a day infinitely in the past and the present day, Aquinas must explain an error about the measuring of time that is contained in the objection. To measure time we must always select two distinct moments of time, and measure the duration from one to the other. Between any two moments the interval must, as the objector realizes, be finite. When the objector urges that we pick a day "infinitely in the past," he is proposing what is inherently contradictory. To pick a day in the past, i.e., a moment that is measurable with respect to the present moment, is necessarily to pick a day that is not "infinitely in the past." If it is impossible to traverse an infinite series, then it is impossible to traverse the infinite series (even in the imagination) from the present moment to some infinitely past moment. It is, therefore, impossible to make the supposition that the objector wishes to make, namely, the picking of a day infinitely in the past. The objection, therefore, fails because it depends upon the making of a supposition that is inherently impossible.

III If the world is eternal, there would have been an infinite number of generations of animals. But an infinite number of generations of animals means that there were an infinite number of causes that produced the present generation of animals. An infinite number of causes, however, is impossible. Aquinas responds by distinguishing between causes that are essentially ordered and causes that are accidentally ordered. It is true that there cannot be an infinite number of essentially ordered causes, but it is quite possible that accidentally ordered causes be infinite. The key to understanding the distinction between these two types of ordered causes is to recognize that essentially ordered causes must all exist simultaneously at the precise moment of causing; accidentally ordered causes need not be simultaneous and need not exist at the moment of causing. Thus, the essentially ordered causes of the generation of an animal are the causes that are simultaneously present at the conception of the new animal: the male, the female, the heat from the sun,[99] and whatever other causes are necessary for the act of conception. These causes must be finite in number and all present simultaneously; the absence of any one of them would prevent the conception from taking place. Accidentally ordered causes, on the other hand, need not exist at the time of conception: the previous generations of animals can all be non-existent, at the time of conception, and the conception will still take place. Since accidentally ordered causes do not have to exist at the time of the actual causing, there is nothing to prevent an infinite multiplication of such causes.

IV If the world is eternal, and if men have always existed in the world, there would have been by now an infinite number of men. But an infinite number of men would mean that there are now an actually infinite number of human souls. Since an actual infinity is impossible, the world can not be eternal. This, Aquinas concedes, is the strongest argument against the possibility of an eternal world. It is a judgment he maintains throughout his career; he raises the objection in the final

---

99. Here Aquinas is following Aristotelian embryology – we might think of the heat from the sun as some more general source of energy in the universe.

part of his last work on this subject, his *De aeternitate mundi*. It is the strongest argument precisely because, unlike the arguments about past time, it argues that something *actual* from the past is "left over." Past time is no longer actual, and therefore it makes no sense to speak about an eternal past as an "actual infinity." Human souls, however, are immortal, and hence all the souls of all the men who have ever lived are now actual. If men have existed from all eternity, there would surely now be an actual infinity of human souls.

To such an argument Aquinas' strongest response is (as he says in the *Summa* [1.46.2, ad 8] and in the *De aeternitate mundi*, but not here in the *Sentences*), that the argument about an infinite number of human souls is strictly irrelevant to the question of the possibility of the eternal duration of the world. It would have been possible for God to have created the world as eternal and to have created the species man as having a temporal beginning. The argument, thus, would hold only in the particular case of an eternal world in which men always existed. The general problem, however, is what is most important: could any creature, of any sort, have been created eternally?

Given the particular nature of the argument that Aquinas is analyzing, we may still ask whether it is demonstrative. Is, for example, an actual infinity of immaterial substances, like human souls, possible? In his early works, Aquinas has not decided that an actual infinity of human souls is impossible (*Quodlibetum nonum* 1.1) The most he will say is that it "seems to be more true" that an actual infinity of human souls is impossible. At *Summa theologiae* 1.7.4 sol. he does argue that an actual infinity of human souls is impossible, although there may be some doubt as to whether the argument he gives is really demonstrative. At the end of the *De aeternitate mundi* he remarks that it has not been demonstrated that God could not make an actual infinity of things.

v If the world is eternal, the world would be equal to God, at least in duration, or the world would have to have an infinite power, which is inappropriate to a creature. Aquinas responds by noting that God's eternity is completely different from eternal temporal duration; God's eternity is not successive but is, rather, the perfect, simultaneous possession of all being. An eternity of time, since it is successive and never complete, could not be equal to God's eternity in any way. Likewise, the world, if it existed eternally, would not be like God in having infinite power, for the power through which the world exists is not from itself but from God.

By the end of the fifth article, Aquinas has refuted the two extreme positions: that necessarily the world is eternal and that necessarily it has a temporal beginning. Reason alone, he thinks, cannot conclude definitively to either position. If reason remains silent on the question, and faith were to speak – as Aquinas thinks it does – there would be no possibility of any conflict between the claims of reason and faith on the question of the eternity or the temporal finitude of the world.

ARTICLE SIX

Having explained that the created world did have a temporal beginning and that it is impossible to demonstrate such a temporal beginning, Aquinas turns finally, in Article Six, to an exposition of the revelation of the temporal beginning of the world: *In principio creavit Deus caelum et terram*. The first line of Genesis, however, indicates more than merely the temporal beginning of the world. Aquinas takes *in principio* to mean "in the beginning of time," but he also accepts the traditional gloss that *in principio* means *in Filio Dei* (in/through the Son of God). He explains this gloss by saying that the notion of efficient causality is appropriated to the Father, the notion of exemplary causality is appropriated to the Son, and the notion of conservation is appropriated to the Holy Spirit. Creation, however, is properly the work of the entire Trinity, and thus *in principio* also means *in uno principio effectivo*. In addition, the fact that God created both the heavens and the earth *in principio* means that God could not have created, as some have thought, material beings through the mediation of spiritual creatures. The revelation of *in principio*, therefore, contradicts three errors about creation: the error of those holding the eternity of the world; the error of those holding that there is more than one first principle of the world (e.g., the Manichees); the error of those holding that material beings were created through the mediation of spiritual beings (the emanationists). Thus, Aquinas' preceding discussions of the eternity of the world, of Manicheanism, and of emanationism have prepared the way for the exegesis of *in principio*. The first five articles constitute the theological and philosophical preparation necessary for understanding the first line of Genesis.

The immense achievement of Aquinas is to have explained so much of the Christian teaching on creation in philosophical terms. Nearly everything essential to the Christian idea of creation – the existence of the Creator, the uniqueness of the Creator, the fact that the Creator creates without intermediaries,[100] the fact that the creation is properly out of nothing, the fact that the Creator creates freely – is not only philosophically comprehensible, according to Aquinas, but also philosophically demonstrable. Only one major element of the Christian teaching, the temporal beginning of the world, is not philosophically demonstrable, although it is certainly comprehensible philosophically. In the doctrine of Aquinas, philosophy and theology are perfect working partners: what philosophy can know only incompletely is completed by the revelation of faith. True philosophical knowledge is never rejected by theology, but only perfected and brought to completion.

100. As we have noted, Aquinas, in Article Three of the text we have translated, does not think that reason can definitively exclude creation through intermediaries, although in faith we know that God does not act in this way. By the time Aquinas composes the *Summa contra Gentiles* (and in all works thereafter), he has concluded that creation through intermediaries is philosophically impossible.

Aquinas on Creation

Writings on the "Sentences" of Peter Lombard
Book 2, Distinction 1, Question 1

To investigate this matter, six [articles][1] are required [on the following topics]: **1** whether there is only one principle; **2** whether from that
principle things come forth by way of creation; **3** whether things are
created only by that one principle, or whether they are also created
by secondary principles; **4** whether one thing is able to be the cause
of another in some way other than by way of creation; **5** whether
things have been created from eternity; **6** on the supposition that
things have not been created from eternity, in what way God is said
to have created the heavens and the earth "in the beginning."

ARTICLE ONE □ WHETHER THERE IS ONLY ONE FIRST PRINCIPLE
Objections
It seems that there are several first principles.

1. Because, according to the Philosopher,[2] *On the Heavens* 2.3
(286a23–24), if one of a pair of contraries should be found in nature,
then the other must be, too. But the highest evil is the contrary of the
highest good, just as evil is the contrary of good. Therefore, since
there is a highest good, which is the first principle of all good things,
it seems that there is also a supreme evil being, which is the first
principle of all evil things. There will thus be two first principles.

2. Furthermore, whatever comes to be is either itself the first
principle or comes from some principle, as is said in the *Physics* 3.4
(203b6–7). But some evil thing does come to be in the world. If,
therefore, it is not the first principle (for if it were, the conclusion of

---

1. We have added words or phrases in brackets, throughout the text, to aid the
reader in following Aquinas' presentation.
2. Aquinas refers to Aristotle as "the Philosopher" and to Averroes as "the
Commentator."

this argument would have been reached), it must be from some principle. But it cannot be from something good, because good is destructive of evil and not the cause of it, just as a hot thing is destructive of a cold thing and not the cause of it. For the same reason, if the evil thing is not itself the first principle, there will be some other evil first principle. There cannot, however, be an infinite regress in principles or in causes, as is proven in *Metaphysics* 2.2 (994a1–18). It seems, therefore, that we must come to a first evil thing which is the principle of all evil. And thus the conclusion is reached.

3. If one should say that evil does not have a principle but is something that happens beyond the intention of the principal agent, against this [the objection is that] everything that happens beyond the intention of the agent is by chance and happens for the least part. But evil occurs for the most part, as is said in the *Topics* 2.11 (115b14–19). Therefore, it seems that evil is intended and has an essential principle.[3]

4. Furthermore, the things that come from just one principle are all alike, because what is caused by a principle imitates the principle. But in reality we find a great contrariety[4] and diversity. There must, therefore, be contrary principles for this diversity.

5. Furthermore, the material and the efficient causes are never identical,[5] as is said in the *Physics* 2.7 (198a23–31), nor are the efficient and formal causes numerically the same.[6] But things have

3. If evil has an "essential principle" (*per se principium*), this means a principle whose intention is to produce evil, rather than an accidental principle of evil, whose intention is to produce good but which accidentally produces evil.

4. On Aquinas' understanding of chemistry, the basic elements are only four (earth, water, air, and fire) and they possess properties that are opposed to other properties as contraries. The properties in question are two pairs of contraries: hot/cold and wet/dry. Earth has the properties of being cold and dry, water of being cold and wet, air of being hot and wet, fire of being hot and dry. As all material things are composed of some, at least, of these four elements, all material things have an inherent contrariety, and the world is a diversity of different kinds of material beings.

5. Literally, "matter and agent never fall together in the same thing." Aquinas is referring to two of Aristotle's four causes, the material cause and the efficient cause. He is saying that the material causes (that out of which something is made) and the efficient cause (the maker) are not the same being. In the building of a house, for example, the lumber (material cause) and the carpenter (efficient cause) are different things (i.e., they are different in being).

6. Again, two of Aristotle's four causes. The formal cause is what something is (its structure, its intelligible nature, its kind, its species), and the efficient cause is

formal, material, and efficient principles, and each category should be traced back to one principle, as is proved in the *Metaphysics* 2.2 (994a–994b30). There must, therefore, be several first principles.

On the contrary

1. On the contrary, unity precedes every multitude, because plurality comes to be from unity. If, therefore, many principles are posited, there must be one prior principle for them. But nothing is prior to the first. It is impossible, therefore, to posit several first principles.

2. Furthermore, whatever things are alike in one way but different in another must be composite things. If several first principles are posited, they must be alike in some way, because they are all principles, but they must also differ, because they are many. They must, therefore, be composed. But no composite thing can be first. Therefore, it is impossible that there be several first principles.

3. Furthermore, if there were several first principles, they would either be alike or they would be contraries. If they were alike, either each one would be a sufficient principle by itself, and thus the rest would be superfluous, or each one would be by itself an insufficient principle and all together would be sufficient for causing things. But in this case, they would not be first principles, both because they would lack some unifying principle which would be prior to them all and because each would act by means of something added to its essence, that is, by being conjoined to others, and no such [conjoined] thing is a first principle. If, however, the principles were contraries, [such would be absurd because] every contrary destroys and impedes its contrary. If, therefore, they were of equal power, each one would block the other so that no one would be able to produce an effect. But if one were more powerful than another, it would destroy the other completely. It is therefore impossible that there be several first principles.

Solution

I answer that "first" is said in two ways, namely, first absolutely and first in some category or in some order. If the word is taken in the second way, then there are as many first principles as there are kinds

---

the maker. Aquinas is saying that the maker and what is made are not the same thing (i.e., not the same in being).

of causes, as the first material cause is prime matter, the first formal cause is being, and so on with the rest. By specifying further the different categories of things, different first principles in each category can be found, even if these categories are within the same kind of cause. Thus in liquids, the prime matter is water, and in dry things the prime matter is earth, and in animals it is the semen or the menstruum.

The first principle absolutely, however, can only be one. This is shown in three ways. First, it is shown from the order itself of the universe, whose parts are found to have been ordered to one another, like the parts of the animal in the whole, which serve the purposes of one another. Such a coordination, however, of many parts cannot happen unless the parts are aimed at one goal. There must, therefore, be one supreme final good, which is desired by all.[7] This is the first principle.

It is also apparent from the very nature of things. The nature of being is found in all things, in some more nobly, in others less nobly, such that the natures of the things themselves are not the very being which they have. Otherwise, being would belong to the concept of the quiddity[8] of any thing, which is false, since the quiddity of any thing can be understood without understanding whether the thing exists.[9] Natures must, therefore, have being from something [else], and there must be ultimately a nature which is its own being, otherwise there would be an infinite regress. And this it is which gives being to all, and there can only be one [such being], since the nature of being is of the same meaning in all, according to analogy.

7. If many parts are coordinated to serve one goal or end, such a coordination cannot happen by chance. If it does not happen by chance, then this one goal is really the goal of each of the parts – the goal is the goal of the whole and of each of the parts. If the many parts are each *intelligent*, they can only work toward the goal by understanding it. To understand the goal, however, is to understand the goodness of it and, therefore, to desire it.

8. "Quiddity" here is used as a synonym for "nature." Either term in this context means "what the thing is" or the formal cause of the thing.

9. This sentence expresses a crucial point in Thomistic metaphysics. The being of things, their existence, does not belong to the nature, essence, or quiddity of things. There is nothing about what things are that indicates that they must exist. The being of things is in some way distinct from the essence of things. This fact is true for all creatures and is not true for God.

The unity of the effect requires the unity of its essential cause. And this is the way of Avicenna, *Metaphysics* 8.3.[10]

The third way is from the immateriality of God Himself. The cause that moves the heavens must be a power that is not in matter, as is proved in the *Physics* 8.5 (257a33–258b9). Among immaterial things, there can only be a diversity if the nature of one is more complete and more existent in actuality than the nature of another. That, therefore, which comes at the summit of completeness and the purity of actuality must be only one, from which comes anything that is mixed with potentiality, because actuality precedes potentiality, and the complete precedes the incomplete, as is proved in *Metaphysics* 9.8 (1049b4–1051a3).

There have been three sorts of error on this matter. Some, such as the early natural philosophers, recognized nothing but the material cause. Hence, those among them who recognized several material principles, said that there were several absolutely first principles.[11]

Some, however, along with the material cause also recognized the efficient cause, and they said that the two first agents are contraries. Empedocles, *Physics* 8.1 (250b24–251a5), for example, [called the two first agents] friendship and strife. The opinion of Pythagoras, *Metaphysics* 1.4 (984b32–985a10), 1.5 (985b23–986b8) is in accord with this. Pythagoras divided all beings into two orders, and he attributed one order to "good," as to a principle, and the other to "evil." And from this sprouted the heresy of the Manicheans, who hold that there are two gods, one the creator of good things, of the invisible and incorporeal things, and of the New Testament; the other the creator of visible things, corporeal things, and the Old Testament.

The third error was of those who recognized that there is an agent and material cause, but that the agent is not the source of matter, although there is only one agent. And this is the opinion of Anaxagoras and of Plato, except that Plato added a third principle,

10. Avicenna, *Liber de philosophia prima sive scientia divina* 8.3, ed. S. Van Riet, 3 vols. (Louvain: E. Peeters ; Leiden: E.J. Brill, 1977–1983), pp. 395–397.

11.   Aquinas is alluding to the pre-Socratic natural philosophers, such as Thales, who held that the primal stuff of all reality is water, or Anaximenes who held that it is air. Among those who recognized several first principles was Empedocles, for example, who recognized earth, water, air, and fire as the ultimate material principles. For a translation of and commentary on the fragments of these philosophers, see *The Pre-Socratic Philosophers*, ed. G.S. Kirk, J.E. Raven, and M. Schofield, 2nd ed. (Cambridge: Cambridge University Press, 1983).

namely, the forms separate from things, which he called exemplars. They also held that each of these causes is uncaused by the others but that through all three the world and the things that compose the world were caused.

Replies to Objections

1. To the first it ought to be said that the highest evil is the contrary of the highest good, not *really* but only *verbally*. This is so for two reasons. First, the "highest evil" is not able to exist, because nothing is so evil that there is not something of good in it, at least its own being. Accordingly, the Philosopher says, *Ethics* 4.5 (1126a12–13), that if something completely evil should come about because of the corruption of everything about it, it itself would not be able to exist. Second, nothing is opposed, either as a privative or as a contrary, to that good which is not able to be destroyed or diminished in any way. So it is that any particular evil thing is opposed, not directly to the highest good, but to some particular [limited] good which is negated by it. I mean that something is *directly* opposed to another, when it is opposed to it just because of the kind of thing that it is. The blackness of a hand, for example, is opposed directly to the whiteness of a hand, but indirectly it is opposed also to the whiteness of a wall, not insofar as it is the blackness of this thing or the whiteness of this thing, but insofar as they are simply blackness and whiteness. In this [indirect] way, any evil is opposed to any good, not according to the nature of this thing or of that thing, but according to the general nature of good and evil. If, therefore, the highest evil should be opposed to the highest good, this will be indirectly, because it is not opposed insofar as [the highest good] is the kind of good that it is but insofar as it is good.

2. To the second it ought to be said that evil does not have a cause except accidentally, and this in two ways. In the first way, an agent is said to be an accidental agent of that which is beyond the intention of the agent, because every agent acts for the sake of an end and intends the good which belongs to the end, and no negation[12] is intended, even though a negation is implied by the form which is brought about. Fire, for example, does not intend to negate the form

---

12. We translate *privatio* here as negation. When Aquinas says that no negation is intended, he means that the agent does not intend something negative but rather something positive. The negation results accidentally, beyond the intention of the agent.

of air in the matter, but rather to propagate its own form. But by propagating its own form it does negate the form of air. Likewise, the sinner intends pleasure, which is a good of one part of him, namely, of his concupiscible appetite,[13] and he does not intend the negation of grace.

In a second way an agent is said to be an accidental agent insofar as it removes something preventing something else. What prevents something else is a form or a thing of some sort. Hence whatever removes that thing is said to cause a negation, as he who extinguishes a candle or carries it out of the house is said to cause darkness. Therefore, the dictum, that whatever is is either a principle or is from a principle, should be understood concerning that which is a real thing, but evil is a negation of sorts and does not indicate any positively existing nature.

3.   To the third it ought to be said that if we speak about evil in nature [*malum naturae*],[14] evil can be considered either with respect to the whole of nature or with respect to some individual agent in nature. If with respect to the whole of nature, it is clear that evil is for the least part, because it is only able to exist among those things that are subject to generation and corruption, the whole of which makes up a small amount of the universe in comparison to the heavens, where there is no evil.[15]

---

13.   The concupiscible appetite is the power that human beings and animals have of desiring bodily pleasures, especially the pleasures of eating, drinking, and sexual union.

14.   The phrase "evil in nature" is the translation for Aquinas' *malum naturae*, literally, "evil of nature." The English word, "evil," is not usually applied to nature. An earthquake or a flood might be called a disaster or something very bad, but we would not normally call it "evil," because we apply the word only to human agents. English has "evil" and "bad," but Latin uses *malum* to serve for both. When Aquinas talks of the "evil in nature" he means something bad, destructive, or disastrous; he does not attribute moral qualities to the sub-human.

15.   According to the cosmology that Aquinas accepted, it is only on the earth and in the earth's atmosphere that things are generated and destroyed. Beyond the moon in the entire rest of the universe, the heavenly bodies move but they do not come into existence or go out of existence, and they are not altered in any way (they do not change their shape, color, temperature, etc.). Thus, nothing bad can happen to anything in the vast heavens beyond the moon, and hence "evil" of the natural kind can only occur in the earthly sphere. Aquinas, therefore, concludes that if we think about the universe as a whole, we realize that evil can only occur in a small part of it.

If, however, evil is considered with respect to some individual agent in nature, it is clear that the action of the agent is always in accord with what belongs to its nature, unless it is at some time blocked, and this occurs rarely. From a defect in a thing's nature evil occurs, as in the case of monstrosities that are born.

On the other hand, if we should speak about the evil that implies guilt, which is found in that kind of being that is not determined to act in only one way, that is, in all beings which act from freedom of the will, this [sort of evil] belongs either to a being with a mixed nature or to a being with just one nature. If [we consider this sort of evil as belonging] to a being with just one nature, such as an angel, it is clear that for the most part the operation of angels is in accord with what is proper for their nature and that the sin of angels occurs for the least part.

If, however, [we consider the evil that belongs to a being] of a mixed nature, such as man, who is composed of an intellectual nature and a sensitive nature,[16] this can be considered in two ways. If we [consider] the whole nature of the species, it is clear that for the most part the action of man proceeds according to that nature the activity of which is more varied and the goods of which are more obvious to us. And since the activity of the sensitive nature is ordered to the pleasurable things of the senses, which are more varied than the pleasure of reason, which is more hidden to us who receive our knowledge from sensation, most men, therefore, follow those activities [of the sensitive nature]. From this fact evil occurs to man, not insofar as he is man, because man is not man insofar as he has sensation, but insofar as he has reason.

If some individual of the species is considered, it happens that someone is determined by his own will to follow activities of reason according to the habit of virtue. Such a man will operate well for the most part and will be deficient only for the least part. When, how-

16. Aquinas says that man has a "mixed nature," literally, several natures ([homo] est plurium naturarum). Aquinas does not mean that there are several different natures in man, for man has only one nature, but he means that man has very different powers, such as the power of reason and the power to desire physical pleasures (concupiscible appetite). The power of reason sets man apart from other animals, whereas the concupiscible appetite is found in both animals and in man. Hence, one may say that man is composed of two natures, although in fact human nature is one nature, not two, and it encompasses both the power of reason and the concupiscible appetite.

ever, he clings to his other nature, he becomes as though a stranger [to his own nature], as is said in the *Ethics* 9.4 (1166a10–1166b24). The judgment made about such a man is like the judgment made about animals, in whom there is only the sensitive nature: he will operate for the most part for the good for which he was made, as the lion acts through cruelty, the dog through anger, the pig through excess, and so forth, as Boethius says, *The Consolation of Philosophy* 4.3.[17] Hence it is clear that evil occurs for the least part, whether it is seen in relation to the principle of all nature or to some individual agent.

4. To the fourth it ought to be said that things have a contrariety among themselves in their proximate effects, but nevertheless even contraries are in accord in the ultimate end to which they are ordered when they are harmoniously put together, as is clear in compounds that are composed of contraries. From this it follows that, even though the proximate agents are contraries, the first agent is one, because the agent and the end must be identical, since these two causes coincide in the same being.

5. To the fifth it ought to be said that, although God is not material in any sense, nevertheless the very being which matter has imperfectly, as it is called a being in potency,[18] it has from God and is traced back to Him as to its principle. Likewise also form, which is a part of a thing, is the likeness of the first agent and flows from Him. So it is that all forms are traced back to the first agent as to the exemplar principle. And so it is clear that there is one absolute principle, which is the first agent, the exemplar, and the ultimate end.

17. Boethius, *The Consolation of Philosophy* 4. pr 3, ed. and trans. S.J. Tester (Loeb Classical Library; Cambridge, MA: Harvard University Press, 1973), pp. 334–335.

18. Every physical thing is a composite of matter and form. Matter is the principle of potentiality; form the principle of actuality. That something can potentially be changed it has from its matter; that something actually is what it is it has from its form. Matter and form are both principles of being; hence, matter could be called "being in potency," and form could be called "being in actuality." Furthermore, the whole substantial composite of matter and form must be made to exist, that is, it must be given being (*esse*) by God. There is, thus, a two-fold composition in all physical substances: form and matter are composed to make up the substance; the substance and being are composed to make the substance actually exist.

ARTICLE TWO □ WHETHER THINGS COME FROM THE ONE PRINCIPLE BY WAY OF CREATION

Objections

It seems that nothing can be made by God to go into being by way of creation.

1. Everything which comes to be was possible before it came to be, because if it were not possible to come to be, it is necessary that it could not come to be, and therefore, it would not have been made. But whatever is possible to come to be or to be moved, is possible through a passive potency, which, since it [the passive potency] is not a being existing by itself, must be in some other being, which is in a state of potency. But nothing is a being in potency to something without also being something in act. Therefore, whatever comes to be, comes to be from some being that is actually pre-existing. But no such thing is created, because to create is to make something from nothing, as is said in [Lombard's] text.[19] Therefore, nothing is able to be created by God.

2. Furthermore, in every change there is something from which the change essentially [comes], because every change is between two end-points. But that from which something comes to be essentially must remain in that which comes to be, either as a whole, as when the matter remains in what comes to be (as a knife is made out of iron), or [it remains] in some material way, as when some whole thing is said to be made from some other whole thing (as flesh is made from food).[20] Blackness is not said to come to be from whiteness except accidentally, that is, after whiteness, just as day is also said to come to be from night. If, therefore, being is said to come to be from non-being, the non-being or some part of it, although it does not have a part, must remain in the being, and it must be that it would be simultaneously being and non-being, which is impossible. Therefore, whatever comes to be, comes to be from some being. It seems impossible, therefore, that something be created by God.

---

19. Peter Lombard, *Sententiae in IV libris distinctae* 2.1.1, ed. Ignatius Brady (Rome: Collegium S. Bonaventurae, 1971), 1: 330.

20. If the material out of which something new is made remains *as a whole* in the new thing, we have one kind of change (an accidental change); if the material out of which something new is made remains in some material way (but not as a whole), we have another kind of change (a substantial change), a change in which a whole new thing is made out of an old thing which no longer exists after the change.

3. Furthermore, no enduring thing is simultaneously in a state of becoming and in a state of having been made. While it is becoming, it is not [yet], and when it has been made, it is. It is not simultaneously existent and non-existent. If, therefore, some enduring thing should be caused to be by God, its becoming must be before its being. But making, since it is an accident, cannot exist without a subject.[21] Therefore, everything which comes to be must come to be from something in which there is a making as in a subject. But no such thing is created. Therefore, nothing is able to come to be by way of creation.

4. Furthermore, if creation is something, it must be an accident, since it is not a substance. Every accident, however, is in some subject, but [creation] cannot be in the created thing as in a subject, because the created thing is the result of creation. Hence, the created thing would be prior to creation, insofar as it is the subject of creation, but also posterior [to creation], insofar as it is the result. Therefore, [creation] must be in some matter, out of which the created thing is made; but this is against the meaning of creation. Therefore, creation is nothing.

5. Furthermore, if creation is something, it is either the Creator or a creature. But it is not the Creator, because, if it were, it would exist from eternity and hence creatures would exist from eternity. It is, therefore, a creature. Every creature, however, is created by a creation, and thus there is a creation of creation, and so on, to infinity. But this is impossible, as is clear in *Physics* 5.2 (225b33–226a6), where it is shown that there is not an action of an action into infinity. Creation, therefore, is impossible.

On the contrary

1. On the contrary is what is said in Genesis [1:1]: "In the beginning God created the heavens and the earth."

2. Furthermore, every agent acts insofar as it is in actuality. But what is partially in actuality and partially in potentiality produces a thing only partially, namely, by bringing form into matter. Therefore, since the first being, God, is actual without any potentiality

---

21. The action of making is an accident, that is, it must belong to some subject. There cannot be a making apart from the thing made; the making is an accident, and the thing made is the subject. "Accident" means that which cannot exist on its own, or, must inhere in a subject; "subject" is that which exists on its own and, hence, can be the subject of accidents.

mixed in, it seems that He is able to produce a thing in its entirety, that is, the whole substance of a thing. To do this, however, is to create. It seems, therefore, that God is able to create.

Solution

I answer that not only does faith hold that there is creation but reason also demonstrates it. It is clear, for instance, that whatever is imperfect in some category arises out of that in which the nature of the category is found primarily and perfectly.[22] In [the category of] hot things, for example, [the degrees of] heat arise from fire.[23] Since every thing and whatever is in the thing shares in *being* in some way, and since every thing has imperfection mixed in, every thing must, in its entirety, arise from the first and perfect being. This, however, we call to create: to produce a thing into being according to its entire substance.

It ought to be known, moreover, that the meaning of creation includes two things. The first is that it presupposes nothing in the thing which is said to be created. In this way it differs from other changes, because a generation presupposes matter, which is not generated, but rather which is transformed and brought to completion through generation. In other changes a subject which is a complete being is presupposed. Hence, the causality of the generator or of the alterer does not extend to everything which is found in the thing, but only to the form, which is brought from potency into actuality. The causality of the Creator, however, extends to everything that is in the thing. And, therefore, creation is said to be out of *nothing*, because nothing uncreated pre-exists creation.

The second thing is that non-being is prior to being in the thing which is said to be created. This is not a priority of time or of duration, such that what did not exist before does exist later, but a priority of nature, so that, if the created thing is left to itself, it would

22. Any category or genus of beings is a category because all of the members of it share the same nature. If the members of the category share the same nature but do so to different degrees, then the fact that there are less perfect members indicate that there is a most perfect member. The nature that is shared by all the members of the category – the "nature of the category" – is found in its most perfect instance in one member.

23. Aquinas regarded fire in its elemental, pure form to be the hottest of things. The fire of a burning match or of a camp fire would be a derivative fire and would be less hot than pure fire.

not exist, because it only has its being from the causality of the higher cause. What a thing has in itself and not from something else is naturally prior in it to that which it has from something else. (In this way creation differs from eternal generation,[24] for it cannot be said that the Son of God, if left to Himself, would not have being, since He receives from the Father that very same being which the Father has, which is absolute being, not dependent upon anything.)

Because of these two points, creation is said to be "out of nothing" [*ex nihilo*] in two ways. On the one hand, the negation [in the word "nothing"] denies the relation implied by the preposition "out of" [*ex*] to anything pre-existing. Thus, the creature is said to be "out of nothing" because it is "not from something pre-existing." And this is the first point. On the other hand, the order of creation to a pre-existent nothing remains affirmed by nature, such that creation is said to be "out of nothing" because the created thing naturally has non-being prior to being. If these two points are sufficient for the meaning of creation, creation can be demonstrated and in this way philosophers have held [the doctrine of] creation.

If, however, we should add a third point to the meaning of creation, that the creature should have non-being prior to being [even] *in duration*, so that it is said to be "out of nothing" because it is temporally after nothing, in this way creation cannot be demonstrated and it is not granted by philosophers, but is taken on faith.

Replies to Objections

1. To the first it ought to be said that, according to Avicenna, *Physics* 1.10[25] and *Metaphysics* 6.1,[26] there are two kinds of agents. One is a natural agent, which is an agent involving motion, and the other is divine, which is the giver of being, as was said. Likewise, we must recognize two kinds of act or effect. One is accomplished through the motion of a natural agent, and all such becoming must be preceded temporally not only by active potency but also by passive potency, because motion is the actuality of that which exists in

---

24. "Eternal generation" describes the relation between the Son and the Father in the Trinity: the Son is "eternally begotten" of the Father, not created by the Father. Since the Son is not a creature, it is not true to say that non-being is prior to being in the Son, since the being of the Son and the Father is just the same. The Son is "one in being with the Father" and "not made".

25. Avicenna, *Sufficientia* in *Opera philosophica* (Venice 1508), 19ra.

26. Avicenna, *Liber de philosophia prima* 6.1; ed. Van Riet p. 292.

potency.[27] There is another sort of effect, however, insofar as [something] receives being from the divine agent without motion. Now if this effect should be new, active potency, but not passive potency, must [temporally] precede its being. Such an effect is said to be possible because of the active potency. If, however, the effect is not new, then the active potency does not precede it in duration but only in nature.

2. To the second it ought to be said that creation is not the sort of making that is properly speaking a change, but is rather a certain receiving of being. Hence it need have no essential relation except to the giver of being, and in this way it is not "out of" non-being, except insofar as it is *after* non-being, as night is "out of" day.

3. To the third it ought to be said that no enduring thing is able simultaneously to become and to have been made, if "to become" is taken properly. But there are some expressions that indicate the "having been made" as though it were a "becoming," as when it is said that motion is ended, for at the same time motion "is ended" and "has been ended." And likewise at the same time [something] is illuminated and has been illuminated, because illumination is the end of motion, as the Commentator says, *Physics* 4.[28] And likewise also, substantial form at the same time is received and has been received; and likewise, something at the same time is created and has been created.

If it is objected that before something has been made there is always a becoming in the proper sense of the word, I say that this is true in all things that come to be through motion, as generation follows upon alteration, and illumination follows upon local motion, but it is not so in creation, as was said.

4. To the fourth it ought to be said that creation can be taken actively and passively. If it is taken actively, since creation signifies the divine operation, which is [nothing but] His essence with a cer-

---

27. "Active potency" is the power or ability that something has to be an efficient cause; it is the power to make or to do something. "Passive potency" is the receptive capability or capacity of something; it is the characteristic of a thing that it could be used or that something could be done to it. In terms of the four causes, active potency is the ability to be an efficient cause, and passive potency is the ability to be a material cause. Notice that motion is defined in terms of potency: it is the actuality of that which exists in potency as it is in potency.

28. Averroes, *In Phys.* 4.§129, in *Aristotelis opera cum Averrois commentariis*, 9 vols (Venice: Apud Junctas, 1562-1574) 4: 201ra–b.

tain relation, in this way creation is the divine substance. If, however, it is taken passively, then it is a certain accident in the creature and it signifies a certain reality which is not in the category of being passive properly speaking, but is in the category of relation.[29] Creation is a certain relation of having being from another following upon the divine operation. It is, thus, not inappropriate that it be in the created thing, which is brought into being through creation, as in a subject. In the same way, sonship is in Peter insofar as he receives human nature from his father, but [sonship] is not prior to Peter himself, but rather follows upon the action and motion which are prior. The relation of creation, however, does not follow upon motion, but only upon the divine action, which is prior to the creature.

   5.   To the fifth it ought to be said that, as was said in the First Book [of Aquinas' Writings on the Sentences],[30] when the creature is related to the Creator, the relation is really founded in the creature, but is in God as a mental construct only. Whence the relation implied by the name of creation does not indicate something in the Creator but only in the created thing.[31] Nevertheless, creation need not be created by another creation, because the relation itself is not related to some other thing by another intermediate relation, except by a mental construct, as was said in the First Book. And relations of this sort, since they are only mental constructs, can be multiplied infinitely.

ARTICLE THREE □ WHETHER THE ACT OF CREATING CAN BE DONE BY AGENTS OTHER THAN GOD
Objections
It seems that the act of creating can be done by agents other than God.
   1.   Everything, in fact, which is not produced in being through generation and which comes to be as something new is created. The rational soul does not come into being through generation. It is created, therefore, by whatever causes it to be. The rational soul, how-

---

   29. Aquinas refers to the nine categories of accidents, according to Aristotle's logic: quantity, quality, relation, acting, being acted upon (or being passive), when, where, being in a position, and possessing. Creation in the passive sense would seem to be in the category of "being acted upon," but if this were so it would imply that the creature is something apart from its being created.
   30. Aquinas, *Scriptum super libros Sententiarum Petri Lombardi* 1.8.4.1, ad 3, ed. by P. Mandonnet and M.F. Moos, 4 vols. (Paris: Lethielleux, 1929–1947), 1: 220.
   31. The text followed here is the Parma edition (*Opera omnia*, Parma: Fiaccadori, 1852–1873) rather than Mandonnet's.

ever, comes into being by the power of the [separate] intelligences;[32] for this reason Plato has God saying to the secondary gods, "Take back to yourselves the money that you have lent out," speaking about the rational soul. And likewise in the *Book of Causes*, proposition 3,[33] it is said that the soul has been created through the agency of an intelligence. It seems, therefore, that angels or intelligences are able to create.

2. Furthermore, whatever power a creature is capable of is given to it by the one who is supremely generous. The power of creating, however, can be given to a creature, as the Master [Lombard] says below, book 4, dist. 5.[34] It seems, therefore, that it can be given to some creature that it create.

3. Furthermore, as matter is more resistant to the agent, [so] is it more difficult for something to be made by [the agent]. Now a contrary is more resistant than absolute non-being. It is, therefore, more difficult for something to be made from a contrary than from non-being. A natural agent, however, does make one contrary from another. It seems, therefore, that [a natural agent] would be able also to make something from absolute non-being, and thus is able to create.

4. Furthermore, as things go forth from God, so also are they ordered back to Him. But according to Dionysius, in many places,[35] the law of divinity is that the extremes are never joined together except through intermediaries. It seems, therefore, that the lowest of beings are not immediately created by God, but by intermediate causes.

5. Furthermore, the primary cause never acts upon the effect of the secondary cause, unless it acts with the action of the secondary cause. But God, who is the primary cause of all things, is the Creator of everything. Any secondary cause, therefore, by [means of] which

---

32. The "intelligences" or "separate intelligences" are spiritual beings, like angels, which are able to exert some causality on our world. The intelligences, for example, might move heavenly bodies such as the planets or the stars.

33. *Le Liber de causis* §32, ed. Adrien Pattin (Leuven: Tijdschrift voor Philosophie, 1966) p. 52; *The Book of Causes*, trans. Dennis J. Brand (Niagara, NY: Niagara University Press, 1981) p. 17.

34. Peter Lombard, *Sententiae* 4.5.3; ed. Brady 2: 267.

35. See, for example, *De coelesti hierarchia* 4.3 (PG 3: 179–182); ed. Günter Heil, in Corpus Dionysiacum 2 (Berlin and New York: de Gruyter, 1991), p. 22; trans. editors of the Shrine of Wisdom, *The Mystical Theology and The Celestial Hierarchies of Dionysius the Areopagite*, 2nd ed. (Fintry, Surrey, England: The Shrine of Wisdom, 1965), pp. 33–34.

God creates through His operation, ought to be called a creator. And so the act of creating belongs not to God alone.

On the Contrary

1. On the contrary, John Damascene, *On the Orthodox Faith*, bk. 2, ch. 3,[36] anathematizes all those who say that angels create something, and it would seem to be within their power more than others. It seems, therefore, that the act of creating belongs to God alone.

2. Furthermore, being and non-being are separated by an absolute infinity. To cause motion, however, through an infinite distance requires infinite power, such as only the divine power is. The act of creating, therefore, belongs to divine power only.

Solution

I answer that there are three opinions on this matter. Some philosophers, for instance, have held that from the first cause there comes immediately one first effect, from which thereafter come others, and so forth. Accordingly, they have held that one intelligence is caused by an intermediate intelligence,[37] that the [human] soul is caused by an intermediate intelligence, and that corporeal things are caused by an intermediate spiritual being. This opinion is condemned as heretical, because it gives the honor which is owed to God to a creature. Such an opinion can lead to idolatry.

Hence others have said that the act of creation can be performed by no creature, nor can it be given to a creature, just as infinite power, which the work of creation requires, cannot be given to a creature.[38]

Others have said that the ability to create has been given to no creature, but nevertheless it could have been given. The Master [Peter Lombard] asserts this opinion in book 4, distinction 5.[39]

---

36. Saint John Damascene, *De fide orthodoxa* 2.3 (PG 94: 874); ed. Eligius M. Buytaert (St. Bonaventure, NY: Franciscan Institute, 1955), p. 74; trans. Frederic H. Chase in *Saint John of Damascus, Writings* (New York: Fathers of the Church, 1958), p. 208.

37. That is, by an intelligence intermediate between the intelligence being caused and God.

38. This is the position Aquinas adopts in *Summa theologiae* 1.45.5; see Appendix A, pp. 110–113.

39. Peter Lombard, *Sententiae* 4.5.3; ed. Brady 2: 267.

Each of these last two opinions seems to have some foundation. Since it pertains to the meaning of creation that there be nothing pre-existing, at least in the order of nature, this can be taken either on the part of the Creator or on the part of the creature. If it is taken on the part of the Creator, that action is called creation which is not founded on the action of some preceding cause. In this way it is the action of the primary cause alone, because all action of the secondary cause is founded on the action of the primary cause. Hence, just as it cannot be given to any creature that it should be the primary cause, so it cannot be given to it that it should be the Creator.

If, however, it is taken on the part of the creature, the proper effect of creation is that of which nothing preexists in reality, and this is being. Hence it is said in the *Book of Causes*, proposition 4,[40] that the first of created things is being, and elsewhere in the same book, proposition 1,[41] it is said that being comes through creation and other perfections are added on through formal causality. In composite beings, especially, the being that belongs to them primarily is the being of matter. Taking creation in this way, it is able to be given to a creature so that, by means of the power of the primary cause operating in the creature, some simple being or matter could be produced. In this way, philosophers have held that the intelligences create, although this is heretical.

Replies to Objections

1. To the first it ought to be said that the philosophical authorities should not be accepted in this matter because they have gone astray here. Nevertheless, all of these authorities can be interpreted in this way: they mean that [the intelligences] create souls just insofar as they move the heavenly bodies and so dispose [human] bodies for the reception of souls. This, however, was not their meaning.

2. To the second it ought to be said that whatever can be given to a creature which pertains to the perfection of its nature, is given to it. This, however, is not true about secondary perfections. For example, not every man who is capable of receiving regal dignity is made by God a king. And so it is also with the power of creating, according to those who say that [the power of] creation can be given to a creature.

40. *Liber de causis* §37, ed. Pattin, p. 54; trans. Brand, p. 18.
41. *Liber de causis* §7, ed. Pattin, p. 47; trans. Brand, p. 15.

3. To the third it ought to be said that the resistance of a contrary does not make a difficulty for acting, except insofar as it separates the potency from actuality. As one contrary is more intense, its potency to the other contrary is reduced. That something should be made from non-being, however, requires absolutely more power than that something should be made from a contrary, because in non-being there is absolutely no potency.

4. To the fourth it ought to be said that although the lower beings are brought to the ultimate end through intermediaries, nevertheless the power of the ultimate end is never given to any of the intermediaries such that one of them would be desired as the ultimate end. In the same way, the power of the primary agent, which is the power of creation, cannot be given to any of the secondary principles.

5. To the fifth it ought to be said that the proximate agent, such as the generator, does not operate in this generated thing except by bringing forth form from the potency of matter. The operation of the primary cause, however, extends even to creating matter itself. Hence, the proximate natural agent is only the generator of this thing, but the primary divine agent is the Creator. And from this it is clear that, just as the operation of art is founded on the operation of nature, insofar as nature prepares the matter for the art, so also the operation of nature is founded on creation, insofar as creation provides the matter for nature.

ARTICLE FOUR □ WHETHER SOMETHING OTHER THAN GOD IS
ABLE TO CAUSE ANYTHING

Objections

It seems that nothing other than God is able to cause anything.

1. An agent which acts without an [instrumental] means is a more perfect agent than one that needs a means in its acting. God, however, is the most perfect agent. It seems, therefore, that He produces all things with no [instrumental] means.

2. Furthermore, angels are the most noble of all creatures. But angels are not the efficient causes of things, because one angel is not the cause of another, nor is an angel the cause of a corporeal creature. It seems, therefore, that creatures other [than angels] would be even less likely to be the causes of things.

3. Furthermore, agents from different species do not produce specifically the same effect. But the first individuals of all species

were created immediately by God, on the supposition that the world did not always exist. It seems, therefore, that nothing is able to produce something the same as itself in species.[42]

4. Furthermore, that which does not come from some matter is only able to be made by creation. But forms and accidents do not have a material part of themselves, for if they did there would be an infinite regress.[43] They, therefore, can only be made by creation, with the following result. Every efficient cause of some thing gives to it either substantial or accidental form. These [forms], however, are only produced by creation. Nothing, therefore, is able to be the efficient cause of anything except the Creator, who is God alone, as was said.

5. Furthermore, the efficient cause is never weaker than the effect. Natural agents, however, act only through active qualities, which are accidents. This is shown by the fact that something cannot be a substantial form in one thing and an accidental form in another. Heat,[44] for example, which is an accident in a man, cannot be the substantial form of fire, and so forth. No natural agent, therefore, produces any substantial form.[45] Hence, the same result follows as above.

42. The argument is that natural causes, since they are specifically different from God, must produce effects that are specifically different from those that God produces. But God, at the beginning, produced *all* effects. Therefore, natural causes can produce none of these, and since there are no other effects beyond these, natural agents can produce no effects.

43. If a substantial form or an accidental form had matter in itself, there would be an infinite regress. If the form of a horse, for example, had its own matter, then the whole horse would be a composite of (1) the horse's body, (2) the form of the horse, and (3) the matter of the form of the horse. Since, however, the horse's body *now* requires a form, because no body can exist without form (i.e., an informing principle which makes the thing be what it is), we will have to introduce another form. This new form, however, on the supposition of the argument, will have to have its own matter, again leaving the horse's body without form. Yet another form will then have to be introduced, and it will again have its own matter, and so forth. The same sort of argument could be made about accidents. The general point is that substantial form must be united immediately to prime matter and that accidents, or accidental forms, must inhere immediately in substances.

44. The heat to which Aquinas refers is a kind of power or energy in an animal which is instrumental in all the animal's natural processes.

45. The objection runs as follows. Since natural agents cause their effects through active qualities (hot/cold; wet/dry), which are accidents, the accidents become efficient causes. An accident, being less of a reality than a substance, cannot be the cause of a substance, and hence an accidental form cannot be the cause of a substantial form.

On the Contrary

1. According to John Damascene, *On the Orthodox Faith*, bk. 2, ch. 23,[46] there is a proper operation for every thing. But every thing which has a proper active operation is the cause of something by its own operation. It seems, therefore, that fire by making heat is the cause of heat, and so forth.

2. Furthermore, if God were the immediate cause of all things, one thing would not depend upon another, as effect upon its cause. If such were the case, a thing would not come to be by the agency of one thing rather than by the agency of another. We see, however, from experience that one thing is not made by just anything, but rather man is always generated from the seed of man. The seed of the father, therefore, is the efficient cause of the son.

Solution

I answer that there are three positions on this question. One of which is that God immediately does all things such that nothing else is the cause of anything. Accordingly, they [who hold this position] say that fire does not cause heat but rather God does, nor is the hand moved but rather God causes its motion, and so forth. But this position is foolish, because it does away with the order of the universe and the proper operation of things, and it defies the judgment of our senses.

The second position is of those philosophers who, in order to retain the proper operations of things, deny that God immediately creates all things. Rather, they say that God is the immediate cause of the first created thing, and this is the cause of the second, and so forth. But this opinion is false, because we hold on faith that angels are not creators but only God is the "Creator of all that is visible and invisible."

The third position is that God immediately causes all things and that individual things have their own operations, through which they are the proximate causes of things, not of all things but only of some. According to the faith, as was said, no creature is held to produce another into being by creation, not by its own power nor by the power of another.

---

46. St. John Damascene, *De fide orthodoxa* 2.23 (PG 94: 950); ed. Buytaert, p. 142; trans. Chase, p. 252.

God alone is the immediate cause of all those things which come into being by creation, and these are things that cannot come into being by motion nor by generation. [This is so for three reasons.] First, because of the simplicity of a substance's essence, in the case that the essence is subsistent. Whatever is generated must be composed of matter and form. Thus, neither angels nor rational souls can be generated but only created. (It is otherwise, however, with other forms[47] which, even if they are simple, nevertheless do not have being independently,[48] because they are not subsistent. Hence, the coming into being belongs not to the forms but to the composite [of form and matter] which has a form, which is said to be properly what is generated as something having a form. Forms of this sort are not said to be generated except in an accidental way.)[49] The same argument also applies to prime matter, which underlies generation and, because of its simplicity, is not generated but created.

Second, [some things come into being neither through motion nor through generation] because of the fact that they are not composed of contraries, such as the heavenly bodies. Everything which is generated, on the other hand, is generated from contraries.[50]

47. Such as the substantial forms of material things, like the form of water.

48. The phrase "being independently" is our translation of *esse absolutum*.

49. An angel is a subsistent essence or, in other words, it is simply an existent form. Unlike material things, it is not composed of matter and form. Hence, material things are generated, because a composite of form and matter is generated out of the potency of matter, but an angel, because it is not a composite, cannot be generated. An angel can come into being, therefore, only by being created out of nothing.

50. Whatever is generated is made out of what is *not* that which is made; in this sense, whatever is generated is generated from its contrary: the non-living becomes the living, the non-human becomes the human, and so forth. It is also true to say that the generated thing is composed out of elements that are to some degree mutually repugnant or that are, in their pure states, incompatible with one another. In Aquinas' chemistry, this meant elements that were hot combined with elements that were cold, and elements that were dry combined with elements that were wet. Hence, it was obvious to Aquinas that whatever is generated is liable to degeneration or destruction. The heavenly bodies, however, such as the sun, the moon, the planets, and the stars, did not appear to the ancients and medievals to be undergoing any decomposition. Since they did not think that such bodies were liable to decomposition, they concluded that these bodies were not composed of contrary elements, as everything on earth is. Heavenly bodies, thus, moved but were never generated or destroyed. If they did come into being at all, it could only have been by God's creating them from nothing.

Third, [some things come into being neither through motion nor through generation] because of the necessity that generation always generates what is similar in species. For this reason the first members of the species were immediately created by God, such as the first man, the first lion, and so forth. Man, for instance, can only be generated from man. It is, however, otherwise with those things which are not generated by an agent that is similar to them in species. For these, rather, the power of celestial bodies along with appropriate matter is sufficient, as, for example, those things which are generated by putrefaction.[51]

Now a creature is able to be the cause of the things that are produced through motion and generation, either because it exerts causality over an entire species, as the sun is the cause of a man and of a lion, or because it exerts causality on only one individual, as man generates man, and fire generates fire. Nevertheless, God is also the cause of these things, operating more intimately in them than do the other causes that involve motion, because He Himself gives being to things. The other causes, in contrast, are the causes that, as it were, specify that being. The entire being of any thing cannot come from some creature, since matter is from God alone. Being, however, is more intimate to anything than those things by which being is specified. Hence, it [being] remains even if those other things are removed, as is said in the *Book of Causes*, proposition 1.[52] Hence, the operation of the Creator pertains more to what is intimate in a thing than does the operation of any secondary causes. The fact, therefore, that a creature is the cause of some other creature does not preclude that God operate immediately in all things, insofar as His power is like an intermediary that joins the power of any secondary cause with its effect. In fact, the power of a creature cannot achieve its effect except by the power of the Creator, from whom is all power,

51. Aquinas, following the ancients, thought that worms, for instance, could be generated from the rotting of garbage. The garbage had to have the appropriate matter (the right active and passive qualities) and the action of a celestial body (the sun) was required. The biology here is incorrect, of course, but the philosophical point is what is important. Aquinas is saying that animal and plant generation need not, in principle, always take place from parent members of the species. That such, in principle, could happen is needed for a doctrine of evolution. Aquinas, of course, did not hold a doctrine of evolution, but the point that he is making here is important if his philosophy is to be held to be compatible with a doctrine of evolution.

52. *Liber de causis* §11, ed. Pattin, p. 48; trans. Brand, pp. 15–16.

preservation of power, and order [of cause] to effect. For this reason, as is said in the same place of the *Book of Causes*,[53] the causality of the secondary cause is rooted in the causality of the primary cause.

Replies to Objections

1. To the first it ought to be said God makes use of other causes for creating, not from need, but from His goodness, for He wishes to give the power of causing to others also.

2. To the second it ought to be said that, if we suppose, according to the opinion of some, that the angels help God by moving the heavenly bodies, it is plain that angels are the cause of generation and corruption through the motion of the heavenly bodies. Even if this causality is not exercised by all angels, nevertheless it involves all of them, because, according to Dionysius, *On the Celestial Hierarchy*, ch. 3,[54] the higher angels instruct the lower angels as to the duties they are to perform. If, however, this supposition is not made, it could be said that, from the fact that angels are more noble, it does not follow that they have the power to cause generation and corruption in things; rather [what follows is that angels have] a higher power, which consists in the knowing of God.

3. To the third it ought to be said that the specifically same effect cannot come immediately from different agents which have determinate operations to determinate effects, for example, art and nature [cannot produce specifically the same effect].[55] But God does not have an operation that is determined to some [one] effect. Rather, by one operation alone, He is able to produce all effects that He wishes to produce. Hence, God, without the operation of nature, is able to make the same effect specifically that nature produces.

4. To the fourth it ought to be said that there are three opinions on the coming to be of things through generation. First is the position of those holding a "hiddenness," such as Anaxagoras, *Physics* 1.4 (187a21–187b7), who held that all things are in all things, and genera-

53. *Liber de causis* §16, ed. Pattin, p. 49; trans. Brand, p. 16.

54. Dionysius, *De coelesti hierarchia* 3.3 (PG 3: 165–168), ed. Heil, pp. 19–20; trans. editors of the Shrine of Wisdom, pp. 30–31.

55. An agent that has a determinate operation to a determinate effect will always produce that effect and will not produce some other. Fire, for example, will always produce heat. It will not produce cold.

tion comes about by drawing one [hidden] thing out of another.[56] Thus, he did not hold true generation, which occurs when a new substantial form is acquired in matter. Into this error also falls the opinion of all the old philosophers who held, not true generation, but that generation occurs by gathering and separating [things] or by altering them. This error arises because they do not recognize a formal cause, but only a material cause, or a material and efficient cause only.

Another opinion, opposed to this one, is that of Plato, who held that there are separated forms, which he called "Ideas," that cause forms to exist in matter. The opinion of Avicenna may be reduced to Plato's, because Avicenna, *On the Progression of Being*, ch. 4,[57] says that all forms are from a [separate] intelligence and that the natural agent merely prepares matter to receive form. This opinion derives from the fact that he thinks that everything is generated from that which is like itself, even though this often does not happen in nature, as in the case of those things that are generated by putrefaction, and also from the fact that he thinks that what is generated is form. This, however, cannot be, because generation essentially is aimed at what has being, for that is the end of any making, and this is only the composite, not the form nor the matter. Hence, form is generated only accidentally.

Third is the opinion of Aristotle, *Metaphysics* 8.1 (1042a24–31), 12.2–3 (1067b7–1070a9), intermediate between these other two, which is that all forms are potentially in prime matter, but they are not actually there, as those who held the "hiddenness" doctrine said. The natural agent produces not the form but the composite, by bringing form from potentiality to actuality. This natural agent by its own action is, as it were, an instrument of God Himself who, as agent, both makes the matter and gives it the potency for form. Hence, if Aristotle's position is held, it is not necessary that the [natural] agent

56. Anaxagoras' position is that there are little bits of everything hidden in everything. Thus, for example, the food that a man eats becomes his bones and flesh because there are little bits of bone and flesh hidden in the food that he eats. The food does not substantially change into bone and flesh; the bone and flesh already present, but hidden, in the food are simply added to the man's bones and flesh.

57. Avicenna, *De causis primis et secundis et de fluxu qui consequitur eas*, in Roland de Vaux, *Notes et texts sur l'Avicennisme latin aux confins des XIIe et XIIIe siècles* (Paris: Vrin, 1934), pp. 97–102; *Opera omnia*, 65ra–b.

create the form or that it make anything from nothing, because it does not make the form but the composite.

5. To the fifth it ought to be said that just as natural heat acts by the soul's power or as an instrument of the soul, as is said in *On the Soul* 2.4 (416b17–30), because it not only causes heat but also contributes to the generation of living flesh, so also the active quality acts by the power of the substantial form. Hence by that action matter is not only brought to the actuality of accidental form but also to the actuality of substantial form.

ARTICLE FIVE ☐ WHETHER THE WORLD IS ETERNAL
Objections
It seems that the world is eternal.

To show this, arguments can be made about the nature of the heavens [objections 1–4], about time [objections 5–7], about motion [objections 8–10], and about the agent or mover [objections 11–14].

1. [The following arguments are about] the nature of the heavens. Whatever is ungenerated and incorruptible has always existed and will always exist. Prime matter, however, is ungenerated and incorruptible, because whatever is generated is generated from a subject, and what is corrupted is corrupted into a subject. There is no subject, however, of prime matter.[58] Therefore, prime matter always existed and always will exist. Matter, however, is never stripped of form. Matter, therefore, has existed eternally, perfected by the forms by which the species are constituted. The universe, therefore, of which these species are parts, has existed eternally. This is the argument of Aristotle in *Physics* 1.9 (192a25–33).

2. Furthermore, what does not have a contrary is neither corruptible nor generable, because generation is from a contrary and corruption is to a contrary. The heavens, however, do not have a contrary, since nothing is opposed to their motion. Therefore, the heavens are neither generated nor corrupted; they, therefore, have always

---

58. A subject is that which independently exists; in this world, subjects are substances composed of form and matter. When generation occurs, a new subject or substance comes into being; when corruption occurs, a subject ceases to exist. Prime matter is neither the subject that ceases to exist nor the subject that begins to exist. It itself is neither generated nor corrupted but underlies the change from one subject to another.

existed and will always exist. This is the argument of the Philosopher, in *On the Heavens*, 1.3 (270a13–23).[59]

3. Furthermore, according to the faith, the substance of the world is considered to be incorruptible.[60] But whatever is incorruptible is ungenerated. The world, therefore, is ungenerated. Proof of the minor premise. Whatever is incorruptible has the power to exist always. But that which has the power to exist always is not found to be sometimes existent and sometimes non-existent, because [if it were] it would follow that at the same time it would be existent and non-existent. This is so because something is existent for the entire time for which its power of existing lasts. Hence, if it has the power to exist for all time, it exists for all time, but if it should happen to be non-existent at some time, it follows that it would simultaneously exist and not exist. No incorruptible thing, therefore, is sometimes existent and sometimes non-existent, but every generable thing is of this sort. Therefore, [the world is not generated]. This is the argument of the Philosopher in *On the Heavens* 1.12 (281 b32–282a13).

4. Furthermore, whatever exists somewhere, where before there was nothing, exists in that which was a void before, because the void is that in which a body can be when nothing is there now. If the world, however, has been made from nothing, where the world is now there was nothing before. Therefore, before the world, there was a void. A void, however, is impossible, as is proven in *Physics* 4.6–9 (213a12–217b28). Also many sense experiences with different powers of sensation show that nature does not allow a void. It is, therefore, impossible, that the world began to exist. This is the argument of the Commentator in *On the Heavens* 3.29.[61]

5. The same thing can be argued about time, as follows. Whatever is always at its beginning and at its end has always existed and always will exist, because there is [always] something after the beginning and before the end. Time, however, is always in that which is the beginning and the end of time, because there is nothing real of time except the present moment, the definition of which is

59. See also Averroes, *In De caelo*. 1, §20, in *Aristotelis opera cum Averrois commentariis* 5: 14v–15r.

60. Aquinas means that the world will continue on in existence. See *In Phys.* 8.2, ed. P.M. Maggiòlo (Turin: Marietti, 1954), §986.

61. Averroes, *In De caelo*. 3, §29, in *Aristotelis opera cum Averrois commentariis* 5: 199r–200r.

that it is the end of the past and the beginning of the future. It seems, therefore, that time always existed and always will exist, and therefore also motion, the movable thing, and the whole world. This is the argument of the Philosopher in *Physics* 8.1 (251b10–28).[62]

6.   Furthermore, whatever can be shown to be never at rest but always flowing has something before itself from which it has flowed. The present moment, however, can be shown to be never at rest, like a point, but always flowing, because the entire meaning of time is to be found in flowing and in succession. Therefore, before any present moment there must have been a previous moment; it is therefore impossible to imagine that time had a first moment. Time, therefore, has always existed, and [the conclusion follows] as before. This is the argument of the Commentator, in the same text.[63]

7.   Furthermore, the Creator of the world precedes the world either in nature only or in both nature and duration.[64] If the Creator precedes the world in nature only, as the cause precedes its effect, then whenever the Creator exists the creature exists, and in this case the world will have existed from eternity. If the Creator precedes the world in both nature and duration, then, because priority and posteriority in duration implies the reality of time, there was time before the existence of the entire world. But this is impossible, because time is a property of motion and does not exist without motion. It is impossible, therefore, that the world has not always existed. This is the argument of Avicenna in his *Metaphysics* 9.1.[65]

8.   The same thing can also be shown from a consideration of motion. It is impossible that there be a new relation between two things unless a change comes about in one of them. This is clear in

62. See also Averroes, *In Phys.* 8.1, §11, in *Aristotelis opera cum Averrois commentariis* 4: 346v–347r.

63. Averroes, *In Phys.* 8.1, §11–12; *Aristotelis opera cum Averrois commentariis* 4: 346v–347r.

64. The Creator *precedes* the world in at least one of two senses. If He precedes the world *in nature*, this means that His nature is first or highest in perfection; but it does not mean that He exists temporally before the world. If He precedes the world *in duration*, this means that the world had an absolute temporal beginning such that the Creator would have existed "before" the world, although there could not have been time before the world, properly speaking. Since the Creator, no matter what is true about the temporal beginning of the world, is the first or highest in perfection, there are only two possibilities: either He precedes the world in nature only or in both nature and duration.

65. Avicenna, *De philosophia prima* 9.1, ed. Van Riet 2: 434–446.

the relation of equality, for example, because two things do not begin to be equal unless one of them is either increased or decreased. Motion, however, always implies a relation of the mover to the thing moved, which are relative to one another. It is therefore impossible for motion to be new unless some change should precede it, either in the mover or in the thing being moved. For example, the two must be brought together, or something of this sort. Therefore, there is always motion before motion, and hence motion, the movable thing, and the world exist from eternity. This is the argument of the Philosopher in *Physics* 8.1 (251a8–251b9).

9. Furthermore, whatever is sometimes in motion and sometimes at rest is ultimately caused by some continuous motion which is perpetual. A succession of the sort which alternates between motion and rest cannot be caused by something that always remains the same, because what always remains the same always causes the same thing. The cause of this succession, therefore, must be some motion which, if it does not exist always, must have some preceding motion. Since there cannot be an infinite regress, there must be some motion that is perpetual. Hence, the same [conclusion follows] as before. This is the argument of the Commentator in *Physics* 8.[66] The same argument can also be found in the words of the Philosopher.[67] The Commentator also invokes this argument, in *Metaphysics* 7,[68] to show that, if the world had been made, this world must have been part of another world, by the motion of which the change in this world was brought about, whether it was a change between motion and rest or between being and non-being.

10. Furthermore, the generation of one thing is the corruption of another. Nothing, however, would be corrupted if it were not generated first. Therefore, before every generation there was a generation, and before every corruption a corruption. But this could not have been if the world were not existent. The world, therefore, always existed. This is the argument of the Philosopher in *On Generation and Corruption* 2.10 (336a14–31).

11. The same thing is able to be shown about the mover or the agent. Every action or motion that comes from an unmoved agent or

66. Averroes, *In Phys.* 8, §9; in *Aristotelis opera cum Averrois commentariis* 4: 344v–345v.

67. Aristotle, *Physics* 8.1 (251a8–251b10).

68. Averroes, *In Phys.* 8, §47, in *Aristotelis opera cum Averrois commentariis* 4: 388v; contrary to the text, the argument is in fact found in the reference just cited.

mover must be perpetual. The first agent or mover, however, is completely unmoved. Therefore, His action and motion must be perpetual. The first premise is proved thus. Whatever acts or causes motion, after not acting or not causing motion, goes from potency to actuality, because everything acts only insofar as it is in actuality. Hence, if it acts after not acting, something about it must now be in actuality which was previously in potentiality. But whatever goes from potency to actuality is moved. Therefore, whatever acts after not acting is moved. This argument can be taken from the words of the Philosopher in *Physics* 8.4 (255a20-255b31).

12. Furthermore, God acts either by free will or by natural necessity. If He acts by natural necessity, since such causes are determined to one effect, the same effect must always be caused by Him. Hence, if the world were made at any time by Him it is necessary that it be eternal. If, however, He acts by free will, no will begins to do something new unless there was some change in the one possessing the will, either because something previously blocking the will has now ceased to do so, or because something now persuades the will to act which was not persuading it before. Since, therefore, the will of God remains immovably the same, it seems that He does not begin to do something new. This argument is common to the Philosopher, in *Physics* 8.1 (252a5-252b6), to Avicenna, *Metaphysics* 9.1,[69] and to the Commentator.[70]

13. Furthermore, for every volitional agent, which sometimes acts and sometimes does not act, a succession of time must be imagined, so that the time when it wills to act can be distinguished from the time when it wills not to act. But to imagine a succession of time requires some kind of change, either on the part of the imagination or, at least, on the part of the thing imagined, because a succession of time is caused by a succession of motion, as is clear in *Physics* 4.11 (218b21-219a10). It is, therefore, impossible that the will begin to cause some new motion which is not preceded by some other motion. This is the argument of the Commentator in *Physics* 8.[71]

14. Furthermore, the will to bring about an effect immediately produces that effect, unless something is lacking to the chosen action

69. Avicenna, *De philosophia prima* 9.1, ed. Van Riet, 2: 442-443.
70. Averroes, *In Phys.* 8, §8 and 15, in *Aristotelis opera cum Averrois commentariis* 4: 343v-344v, 349v-351r.
71. Averroes, *In Phys.* 8, §15, in *Aristotelis opera cum Averrois commentariis* 4: 349v-351r.

which might come later. For example, if I now will to make a fire tomorrow when it will be cold, coldness is now lacking to prevent my chosen action, but as soon as the coldness comes I will make the fire, unless something else prevents me. God, however, has the eternal will to make the world, otherwise [His will] would be mutable. It is, therefore, impossible that He should not have made an eternal world, except in the case that something should have been lacking to the world which later came forth. Nothing, however, could come forth except through some action. Therefore, before this [world] was made as something new, there must have been some action that produced a change. Hence no new thing could be caused by an eternal will unless it were aided by some eternal motion. Therefore, the world must have existed eternally. This is the argument of the Commentator, in the same place.[72]

On the Contrary
[Arguments to show that the world necessarily had a temporal beginning]
1.   God either is the cause of the substance of the world, or He is not and is the cause of its motion only. If [God is the cause] of the motion only, then the substance of it [the world] has not been created. [The world] is, therefore, a first principle, and hence there will be several first principles and several uncreated things, which was argued against above [Article One]. If, however, He is the cause of the substance of the heavens, giving being to the heavens, since whatever receives being from something follows it in duration, it seems that the world did not always exist.

2.   Furthermore, every created thing has been made from nothing. But whatever has been made from nothing is a being after it was nothing, since being and non-being cannot be at the same time. Therefore, the heavens must first have not existed and then later existed, and the same for the whole world.

3.   Furthermore, if the world existed from eternity, then an infinite number of days have preceded this day. An infinite number of things, however, cannot be gone through. Therefore, it would never have been possible to arrive at this [present] day. But that is false. Therefore, etc.

72. Ibid.

4. Furthermore, whatever can be added to can be greater or less. But to the days that have passed there can be the addition of days. Therefore, past time can be greater than it is. But there is nothing greater than the infinite, nor can there be. Therefore, past time is not infinite.

5. Furthermore, if the world existed from eternity, then there was also generation from eternity both of men and of animals. But every generation requires a parent and an off-spring, for the parent is the efficient cause of the off-spring. Thus there is an infinite regress in efficient causes, which is impossible, as is proven in *Metaphysics* 2.2 (994a1–994b31). It is impossible, therefore, that there was always generation and the world.

6. Furthermore, if the world always existed, there were always men. Therefore, an infinite number of men have died before us. But when each man dies his soul does not die but lives on. There are, therefore, now actually an infinite number of souls separate from bodies. But it is impossible that there be an actual infinity, as is proven in *Physics* 3.5 (204b10–206a8). It is, therefore, impossible that the world have always existed.

7. Furthermore, it is impossible that something be equal to God. But if the world always existed, it would be equal to God in duration. This, therefore, is impossible.

8. Furthermore, no finite power can perform an infinite operation. But the power of the heavens is a finite power, since the quantity [of the heavens] is finite, and it is impossible that there be an infinite power in a finite quantity. It is, therefore, impossible that the motion [of the heavens] exist for an infinite time, and likewise impossible that their existence could last for an infinite time, because the duration of a thing does not exceed the power that it has for existence. Hence, [the heavens] began to exist at some time.

9. Furthermore, no one doubts that God precedes the world by nature. In God, however, His nature and duration are the same. God, therefore, preceded the world in duration. The world, therefore, did not exist from eternity.

Solution

I answer that there are three positions on this question. First [is the position] of the philosophers, who have said that not only is God eternal but so also are other things. But [they have said this] in different ways. Some, before Aristotle, have held that the world is generable and corruptible and that, what is true of an individual in a species, that one individual is corrupted and another is generated, is true of the entire universe. This was the opinion of Empedocles. Others have said that things were dormant for an infinite time and that they began to be moved by an Intellect which drew them out and separated one thing from another. This was the opinion of Anaxagoras. Others have said that things were eternally in a random motion and that, at some time, they were brought into order, either by chance, as Democritus thinks that indivisible self-moving bodies form compounds by chance, or by a creator, which Plato thinks, as is said in *On the Heavens* 3.2 (300b9–26). Others have said that things existed eternally in just the way that they do now, and this is the opinion of Aristotle and of all the philosophers who follow him. This last opinion is the most probable of the opinions just given, but they are all false and heretical.

The second position is of those who say that the world and everything other than God began to exist after they had not existed, and that God could not have made an eternal world, not because of a lack of His power, but because the world could not have been made eternally since it was created. They also maintain that the fact that the world began to exist is not only held on faith but can also be proven by a demonstration.

The third position is of those who say that everything other than God began to exist, but nevertheless the fact that the world has begun to exist cannot be demonstrated but is rather held and believed to be so by divine revelation. This position rests upon the authority of Gregory [the Great], who says, in *Homilies on Ezekiel*,[73] that some prophecy concerns the past as when Moses prophesied when he said in Genesis,[74] "In the beginning God created the heavens and the earth." And I agree with this position, because I do not believe that we are able to formulate a demonstrative argument for this, just as [we are not able to formulate a demonstrative argument] for the [existence of] the Trinity, although it is impossible that the Trinity not exist. In confirmation of this is the weakness of the arguments given as demonstrations, all of which have been taken up and refuted by the philosophers who maintain the eternity of the

73. Gregory, *Homiliae in Hiezechihelem prophetam* 1.1.1 (PL 76: 786; CCSL 142: 6).

74. It was the commonly accepted view in the Middle Ages that Moses was the author of the first five books of the Bible.

world. If someone should try to prove the newness of the world by relying on such arguments against the philosophers, his arguments would become rather a mockery of the faith than a confirmation of it.

I say, therefore, that there are demonstrations for neither side of the question but probable or sophistical arguments on both sides.[75] The Philosopher's words indicate this when he says, *Topics* 1.11 (104b16), that there are certain problems for which we have no argument, such as whether the world is eternal. Hence, he himself never intended to demonstrate this, as is clear from his way of proceeding. Whenever he treats this question he always adds some kind of rhetorical argument, either by appealing to the opinion of the many or to the probability of his arguments, which is completely inappropriate for someone giving a demonstration.

The reason this question cannot be demonstrated is that the nature of a thing is quite different in its complete being from what it was when it was in its process of being made by its cause. For example, the nature of a man who is already born is different from that of the man while he is still in his mother's womb. Hence, if someone should argue on the basis of the full-grown man what must be true of the man in an incomplete state in the womb of his mother, he would be deceived. Accordingly, Rabbi Moses, *The Guide of the Perplexed*, ch. 17,[76] tells the story of a certain boy whose mother died in his infancy, who was raised on a solitary island, and who, at the age of reason, asked someone whether and how men were made. When the facts of human generation were explained to him, he objected that such was impossible, because a man could not live without breathing, eating, and expelling wastes, so that it would be impossible for a man to live for even one day in his mother's womb, let alone nine months. Like this boy are those who, from the way that things happen in the world in its complete state, wish to show either

75. A demonstration is an argument that produces scientific knowledge, that is, knowledge which is necessarily so and cannot be otherwise. No reasonable person can deny the truth of such an argument. A probable (or dialectical) argument is an argument that produces, not knowledge, but opinion. Since opinions, even if true, are not *necessarily* true, a reasonable person can deny the conclusions of such arguments. A sophistical argument is not a real argument at all but only an apparent argument. It is a defect of reasoning, with premises that may be false, with a conclusion that may be false, and with no proper logical order of premises to conclusion.

76. Moses Maimonides, *The Guide of the Perplexed*, 2.17, trans. Shlomo Pines (Chicago: University of Chicago Press, 1963), pp. 294–298.

the necessity or the impossibility of the beginning of the world. What now begins to be begins through motion; hence what causes motion must always precede [the motion] in duration and in nature, and there must be contraries; but none of these are necessary in the making of the universe by God.

Replies to Objections [which conclude that the world is eternal]

1. To the first, therefore, it ought to be said that matter is ungenerated and incorruptible, but it does not follow that it has always existed. The reason for this is that it began to exist, not through generation from something but from absolutely nothing. Likewise, the world could cease to exist, if God should will it, by whose will being is given to matter and to the entire world.

2. And likewise it ought to be said to the second that that argument applies to a beginning [brought about] by generation and motion. Hence that argument is against Empedocles and others who have maintained that the heavens are generated.

3. To the third it ought to be said that the potency for existing which now exists in the heavens is not limited to some finite time, and hence if the heavens should always have [the potency], they are able to exist because of it for an infinite time in the past and future. The heavens, however, have not always had this potency of existing; rather, it was given to them by the divine will in creating them.

4. To the fourth it ought to be said that before the creation of the world there was no void, as there is none after, because the void is not a simple negation but a privation. Hence, in order that there be a void, as those who suppose that there is one would say, there must be a place or real dimensions, neither of which did exist before the world. And if it should be said that [the existence of the world] was possible [before the world actually did exist], I say, as was said above [Article 2, Reply to 1], that [this possibility] existed nowhere but in the power of the agent.

5. To the fifth it ought to be said that the argument is circular, as is clear according to the Philosopher. The prior and posterior in time come from the prior and posterior in motion. Thus, when it is said that every present moment is the end of the prior and the beginning of the posterior, the supposition is that every part of motion follows some motion and precedes another. Hence, I say the proposition cannot be proven except on the supposition of that which is concluded through it. It is thus clear that it is not a demonstration.

6. To the sixth it ought to be said that the present moment is never understood as something at rest but as always flowing. It is not, however, flowing from something prior, unless a motion should precede it, but it is flowing to something posterior; or, on the other hand, it is not flowing into something posterior, unless a motion should follow, but it is flowing from something prior. Hence, if a motion never followed or preceded, the "present moment" would not be the present moment. This is plain in any motion which is seen to have had a beginning. Any part of it is flowing, but nevertheless there is a beginning and an end, the end-point from which [*terminus a quo*] and the end-point to which [*terminus in quem*].

7. To the seventh it ought to be said that God precedes the world not only in nature but also in duration, not, however, in a duration of *time*, but in a duration of *eternity*. Before the world there was no time in reality, but in imagination only, because we now imagine that God could have added many years earlier to this finite time, and to all of these earlier years God's eternity would have been present. In this way it is said that God could have made the world before He had made it, or [He could have made it] greater or [He could have made] more [worlds].

8. To the eighth it ought to be said that a new relation comes about not from a change in the mover but from a change in the thing moved, if we take creation as a change in the broad sense of the term, although properly it is not a change, as was said above [Article 1, Solution]. Hence, the creation of the heavens precedes its motion, at least by nature, although no motion precedes creation, since it is from non-being absolutely. Nevertheless, if it should be supposed that the heavens had existed before they began to be moved, still the argument [objection 8] would not be sound, because two kinds of relations must be recognized.[77]

77. Suppose that the heavens existed for a time before they were caused to move. If they began to move after not moving, would such a beginning imply a new relation between mover and thing moved and hence a change in the mover, that is, in God? No, says Aquinas, but to see why he must distinguish two sorts of relation. In order to understand relations in general, let us recognize that the *subject* is that which is related; the *term* is that to which the subject is related, and the *foundation* is that with respect to which the subject is related (or the cause of the relation). Carroll, for example, is six inches taller than Baldner. Carroll is the subject of the relation, Baldner is the term, and the quantity, six inches, is the foundation. This is an example of the first sort of relation that Aquinas discusses. In this sort of relation, the relation can be new if there is a change either in the subject or in the

One kind of relation is absolute, as in all things which are related to something else in being, such as fatherhood and sonship. Such a relation is not made new except through the acquisition of that upon which the relation is founded. Hence if it is acquired through motion, the relation follows upon motion, as, for example, the likeness of one thing to another follows upon an alteration in the quality upon which the relation is founded. If, however, the relation is acquired through creation, it follows upon creation, as, for example, the likeness of the creature to God is founded on the goodness which is acquired through creation, by which the creature is compared to God.

Other kinds of relative things are those which at the same time imply the relation and the foundation of the relation. A newness, moreover, in such relations requires the acquisition of the very thing which is signified by the name, as, for example, the habit [of the intellect] which is science. It is likewise with the relation implied by the name "motion," which is made new by the acquisition of that motion which is caused by the mover in the thing moved.

9.   To the ninth it ought to be said that the efficient cause of the sort of alternation between the world's not existing and later existing is not some motion, but is rather a thing that always remains the same, namely, the divine will, which has willed from eternity that the world should go into being after non-being. And if it should be said that the same thing always makes the same thing, I say that this is true for an agent if "agent" is taken in the strict sense of the term, meaning that it produces precisely just this effect. For example, a

---

term: either Carroll becomes shorter or taller, or Baldner becomes shorter or taller. If that happens, both the subject and the term are in a new relation. With the second sort of relation, however, in order for a new relation to occur, there *must* be a change in the subject, but there need not be a change in the term. When a man begins to understand, for example, there must be a change in him, and when a thing begins to move, there must be a change in the thing moved, but there need be no change in the thing that the man understands or in the mover. Hence, the heavens are in relation to God who is the mover, but the new motion of the heavens would not imply necessarily any change in God.

To put all of this another way, the first sort of relation is a genuinely reciprocal relation (the subject is really related to the term, and the term is really related to the subject), but the second sort of relation is asymmetrical, for the subject is really related to the term, but the term is not really related to the subject. That is why in the second sort of relation, the newness of the relation implies no necessary change in the term, but only in the subject.

natural agent is specified by its proper form so that its action is always in accord with what is appropriate to its form. Likewise, a voluntary agent is specified to action through the proposal of the will. Hence, if the will is not liable to be blocked or moved, the effect of the will follows from the simple proposal of the will. And this is true about the divine will in that, forever remaining the same, it forever accomplishes what it has willed eternally, because it is never blocked [by something else].[78] It does not, nevertheless, make to exist forever what it has forever willed, for it does not will [that something should exist forever]. Hence, if it did accomplish what it itself does not will, it would be as though heat produced cold.

10. To the tenth it ought to be said that the first individuals of those things which are generated and corrupted did not come into being through generation but through creation. Hence, there need not have pre-existed something out of which they were created, and so on, infinitely.

11. To the eleventh it ought to be said that there are two kinds of agent. One kind acts by the necessity of nature, and this kind is de-termined to action through that which is in its nature. It is, accord-ingly, impossible that it begin to act unless it is brought from po-tency to actuality, whether this actuality be essential or accidental. The other sort of agent acts by will, but here a distinction must be made. One sort [of agent that acts by will] acts by means of an action that is not the essence of the agent itself. From such agents, a new effect cannot come forth without a new action, and the newness of action results in some change in the agent, as it goes from rest to activity, as is said in *On the Soul* 2.5 (417a14–417b28). Another sort [of agent that acts by will acts] without any intermediate action or instrument, and such an agent is God. Hence His willing is His action, and since His willing is eternal, so also is His action. Never-theless, His effect is strictly in accord with His will, which proposes that [something] exist or be made in a certain way, and thus [the agent, i.e., God] does not go from potency to actuality, but rather the effect which was in the power of the agent is made to be actually real.

---

78. As it is not caused by anything else, it is not dependent upon anything other than itself to accomplish that which it wills. Hence, the simple proposal of the divine will all by itself is sufficient for it to accomplish what it wills.

12. To the twelfth it ought to be said that for all those agents which act for an end that is beyond their will,[79] their will is guided by that end. Hence [such a will] wills to act at some times and not at others, according to those things that help or impede attaining the end. The will of God, however, did not give being to the universe for the sake of some end existing beyond His own will, just as He does not cause motion for some other end, as the philosophers agree, because the more noble thing does not act for the sake of something less than itself. Therefore, the fact that God does not always cause an effect is not due to something persuading Him to act or preventing Him, but to the determination of His own will, which acts from a wisdom that is beyond our understanding.

13. To the thirteenth it ought to be said that the divine intellect understands all things at once. Thus, from the fact that [God] understands what is the case at this time or at that time does not imply any change in His intellect, although such could not happen in our intellect. It is, thus, clear that the objection is sophistical. Likewise, there is no implication of any motion on the part of a thing imagined, because God has not willed to make the universe after some *time*, because the "time" before was nothing but imaginary, as was said.

14. To the fourteenth it ought to be said that something *was* lacking to the chosen action, and for that reason the divine will has not produced the universe eternally. The suitability of it [the chosen action] to the end is what, in fact, can be understood to be lacking to the chosen act so that it was delayed. The will of a man, for example, delays the taking of medicine when the medicine is not suitable to his health. And so I say that for this universe to have been made eternally it would have lacked the suitability to the end, which is the divine will. God, in fact, has willed that it have being after non-being, both in nature and in duration. If it had been eternal, this [being after non-being in duration] would have been lacking to it. Hence it would not have been suitable to the divine will, which is its end.

79. That is, the end to be attained cannot be accomplished simply by willing that the end be attained. If a student wills to attain a high mark in a class, his mere *willing* that he should receive the grade is not enough. He must also study, attend class, etc.

Replies to the Arguments "On the Contrary" [which conclude that the world necessarily has a temporal beginning]:

Since the philosophers have responded to the arguments given "on the contrary," which I have said are not demonstrations, we, too, should respond to them as the philosophers themselves have done, lest someone attempting to argue against those who maintain the eternity of the world should unwisely rely upon them.

1. To the first, therefore, it ought to be said that, as the Commentator says in *On the Substance of the World*, ch. 2,[80] Aristotle never intended that God was the cause of only the motion of the heavens; [Aristotle also thought] that He was the cause of its substance, giving it being.[81] Since [the heavens] are finite in power, because they are bodily, they require some agent of infinite power who could give them perpetual motion and perpetual being (just as [a cause is needed for] motion, so also for being). Nevertheless, it does not follow that God precedes the heavens in duration, because He does not give being through motion but through eternal causation, insofar as His knowledge is the cause of things. From the fact that He knows, eternal being results, just as, on the supposition that the sun exists eternally, its rays are eternal.

2. To the second, Avicenna responds in his *Metaphysics*, tract. 6, ch. 1 & 2, tract. 9, ch. 4.[82] He says, indeed, that all things have been created by God and that creation is from nothing, that is, the creature has being after non-being. This, however, should be understood in two ways. If it indicates an order of duration, then it is false, but if it indicates an order of nature, then it is true. What a thing has in itself is prior by nature in the thing to what it has from something else. Everything, however, other than God, has its being from another. By nature, therefore, any thing would be non-being, if it did not have its being from God. In this way, Gregory also says, *Magna Moralia* [*Commentary on Job*], bk. 16, ch. 37,[83] all things would fall into nothingness, if the hand of the Almighty did not hold them. Hence, the

---

80. Averroes, *De substantia orbis* 2, ed. and trans. Arthur Hyman in *Averroes' De substantia orbis* (Cambridge, MA: Medieval Academy of America; Jerusalem: Israel Academy of Sciences and Humanities, 1986), pp. 83–87.

81. This is one of several places in which Aquinas claims that Aristotle understands the first cause as a giver of being. See Appendix D, pp. 128–129.

82. Avicenna, *De philosophia prima* 6.2 and 9.4, ed. Van Riet, pp. 303–306 and 476–477.

83. Gregory, *Moralia in Iob* 16.36–37 (PL 75: 1143; CCL 143: 825).

non-being which things have by nature is prior in them to the being which they have from another, even if it is not prior in duration. In this way the philosophers grant that things have been created and made by God.

3. To the third it ought to be said that an actual infinity is impossible, but an infinity in succession is not impossible. Any given part, however, of an infinity in succession is finite, and "going through" can only be understood from one determinate point to another. Since any period of time is taken as something determinate, from one point to another is always a finite time. In this way it is possible to "go through" to the present time.[84] Or it could be said that past time is infinite earlier but finite later, whereas future time is just the opposite. A limit, beginning, or end can be put on anything if it is in some way finite. Hence, according to some, from the fact that past time is infinite, it has no beginning, but it does have an end. Hence it follows that if a man should begin to count days from this day, he could not count to a first day, and the opposite would be true about the future.[85]

4. To the fourth it ought to be said that an addition cannot be made to an entire infinite succession, even if "infinite" is taken as a *potential* infinite, but there can be an addition to some actually finite part. And nothing prevents that finite part from being greater or smaller. That the objection is sophistical is clear from the fact that it would imply also that there can be no addition of infinite numbers, as if one said the following. There are numbers that are greater than ten which are not greater than one hundred. There are, therefore, more numbers greater than ten than are greater than one hundred, and since there are already an infinite number of numbers greater than one hundred, there will be something greater than the infinite. It is clear, therefore, that "greater than," "addition," and "going through," only apply to what is *actual*, whether the actual exists in reality, or whether it exists in the mind or in the imagination. Hence,

---

84. The argument is that it makes no sense to talk about "going through" a period of time, unless we talk about going from one determinate point of time to another determinate point of time. In effect, Aquinas is saying that the objector is guilty of begging the question, for by insisting that one "goes through" a period of time to arrive at the present moment, one is implying already that time is finite, because the notion of "going through" is a notion that is applicable only to a finite period of time.

85. That is, he could not count to a last day.

these arguments sufficiently prove that there is no actual infinity, but none is required for the eternity of the world. This refutation is taken from the words of the Philosopher, *Physics* 3.6, 3.7 (206a9–206b33, 207b27–34).

5.   To the fifth it ought to be said that one effect cannot have an infinite number of essential causes, but it can have an infinite number of accidental causes. In other words, it is impossible that some effect essentially require an infinite number of causes, but it is possible that there be an infinite number of causes which do not essentially bear upon the effect. For example, in order that a knife exist, some efficient causes are essentially required, such as a craftsman and a tool, and it is impossible that these be infinite in number, because there would consequently be an actual infinity of things. If, however, the knife is made by an old craftsman who many times replaces his tools, there would be a successive multitude of tools, [but] this is accidental. Nothing prevents an infinite number of tools from existing which come before this knife, if the craftsman should be eternal.[86] The same is true in the generation of animals, because the semen of the father is the efficient cause and the instrument of the sun's power.[87] Because instruments of this sort, which are secondary causes, are generated and corrupted, it can happen that they are infinite in number. In the same way it can also happen that there were an infinite number of days before this day, because the substance of the sun is eternal, according to them, and each revolution of it is finite. This is the argument of the Commentator in *Physics* 8.[88]

6.   To the sixth it ought to be said that this objection is the strongest of them all, but Algazel responds to it in his *Metaphysics*,[89] where he distinguishes finite from infinite being. He grants that there are an infinite number of actual human souls, but this is accidental, because rational souls separate from bodies have no dependence

---

86. Notice, however, that the making of *this* knife does not depend upon the previous infinite number of tools; the tools actually used in the making of it are only finite in number.

87. For Aristotelian embryology, which Aquinas accepted, animal generation required the agency of both the sun (as a kind of universal cause) and the male parent as a specific efficient cause.

88. Averroes, *In Phys.* 8, §47, in *Aristotelis opera cum Averrois commentariis* 4: 388r–v.

89. Algazel, *Metaphysics* 1.1.6, ed. J.T. Muckle, *Algazel's Metaphysics: A Medieval Translation* (Toronto: St. Michael's College, 1933), pp. 40–41.

upon one another.[90] The Commentator, on the other hand, responds that souls do not remain individually many when separated from the body, but that from all souls there remains one only, as will be clear below.[91] Even if this position, which [Averroes, the Commentator] gives in *On the Soul* 3, had not been disproven earlier, the argument against him would not be conclusive.[92] Rabbi Moses also touches on this argument, *The Guide of the Perplexed* 1.73,[93] when he shows that the given argument is not a demonstration.[94]

7. To the seventh it ought to be said that even if the world always existed, it would not be equal to God in duration, because the divine duration, which is eternity, is a simultaneous whole, whereas the duration of the world is a succession of time. Boethius explains this in *The Consolation of Philosophy*, book 5, prose 6.

8. To the eighth it ought to be said that, according to the Philosopher, in the heavens there is no "potency for existing" but a potency for moving only. A potency for existing, therefore, cannot be said to be either finite or infinite, but the potency for moving is finite. Local motion, however, which is the kind of motion involved with this potency, need not be finite, because motion receives [or would receive] its infinity of duration from the infinity of the moving power, from which motion is given to the movable thing. This is the

90. The impossibility of an actual infinity has been established concerning material things which are essentially related to one another and dependent upon one another. Since souls separate from bodies have no dependence upon one another, even though, on the supposition of the argument, there would be an actually infinite number of them, such an infinity would not be precisely the kind that has been shown to be impossible.

91. Aquinas, *In Sent.* 2.17. 2.1.

92. That is, the argument to show that the world could not have been eternal in the past because such a world would imply an actual infinity of human souls would not be a conclusive argument, even if the position given by Averroes were not disproven. In other words, Averroes cannot be refuted by an argument such as the one given as the sixth objection in "On the Contrary". See Averroes, *Commentarium magnum in Aristotelis libros de anima*, ed. F. Stuart Crawford, (Cambridge, MA: The Mediaeval Academy of America, 1953), pp. 440–443.

93. Maimonides, *The Guide of the Perplexed* 1.73 ["Eleventh Premise"], trans. Pines, pp. 212–213.

94. See Appendix B, pp. 121–122, our translation of *De aeternitate mundi*, where Aquinas gives a slightly different response to the question of an actual infinity of human souls.

argument of the Commentator, in *Metaphysics* 12.[95] Nevertheless, when he says that [the heavens] do not have a potency for existing, this should be understood to apply to the acquiring of being through motion; they do have the power or potency for existing, as is said in *On the Heavens* 1.12 (283a2–24), and this power is finite. Infinite duration, however, is acquired from the infinite separate agent, as he says in the book, *On the Substance of the World*, ch. 3.[96]

9. To the ninth it ought to be said that the duration of God, which is His eternity, and His nature are one thing. They are, however, distinguished intellectually or in their meaning, because "nature" means a kind of causality, as nature is said to be the principle of motion. "Duration," however, means a kind of permanence. Accordingly, if the excellence of the divine nature and duration over the creature is taken as a kind of reality, they are found to be the same excellence. Just as the divine nature precedes the creature in worth and in causality, so also the divine duration precedes the creature in the same ways. Nevertheless, if God precedes the world according to nature, as is meant when it is said that God precedes the world naturally, it is not necessary that He also precede the world according to duration, as is meant when it is said, God precedes the world in duration. This is because "nature" and "duration" have different meanings. Likewise, other similar objections can be answered, as was said in the first book [*In 1 Sent.* 30.1.1–3].

ARTICLE SIX ☐ THE MEANING OF "*IN THE BEGINNING* GOD CREATED THE HEAVENS AND THE EARTH"

Objections

It seems that it is wrong to explain "In the beginning God created the heavens and the earth" to mean "In the Son."

1. The Father is the beginning of the whole divinity, as Augustine says, in book 4 *On the Trinity*, chapter 20.[97] By "beginning," therefore, the Father should appropriately be understood. [98]

---

95. Averroes, *In Metaph.* 12, §41, in *Aristotelis opera cum Averrois commentariis* 8: 323v–325r.

96. Averroes, *De substantia orbis* 3, ed. Hyman, pp. 100–103.

97. Augustine, *De trinitate* (PL 42: 9080; CCL 50: 199–200); *The Trinity*, trans. Stephen McKenna (Washington, DC: Catholic University of America, 1963) , pp. 167–168.

98. The problem for Thomas in Article Six is that the phrase from Genesis 1:1, "In the beginning," *in principio*, can have at least three different meanings. (1) It can

2. Furthermore, as was said in the First Book [of the *Sentences*],[99] *"from* Him" refers to the Father, "*in* Him" refers to the Holy Spirit. It therefore seems that by "*in* the beginning" the Holy Spirit and not the Son is meant.

It also seems that it is wrong [for "*in the beginning*"] *to mean "in the beginning of time".*

3. Time is dependent upon the motion of the firmament, but the firmament was not created until the second day. The beginning of time, therefore, occurred after the creation of the heavens and the earth. [The heavens and the earth], therefore, were not created in the beginning of time.

4. Furthermore, time is one of the four first created things. But there is no time at the beginning of time, because it is impossible that there should be time in an indivisible moment. Neither, therefore, were the heavens or the earth [created at the beginning of time.][100]

It also seems wrong that "in the beginning" should mean "before all things."

5. As is said in the *Book of Causes*, proposition 4, the first of created things is being, and there was nothing else created before it.[101] But the heavens and the earth did not exist before their own being. Therefore, there was something created before the heavens and the earth.

6. Furthermore, in Ecclesiasticus [18:1] it is said, "He who lives forever has created all things at the same time." Therefore, the heavens and the earth were not created before all things.

---

mean "in the principle" or "in the cause." In this sense, the principle or cause would be the Second Person of the Trinity, because from John 1:1, the *principium* is associated with the *verbum*, and the Word is the Son of God. (2) *In principio* can mean, "in the beginning of time," that is, at the very first moment. (3) *In principio* can mean "before other things" -- not necessarily at the first moment, but in a period of time before other things were created. These different senses are possible because the Latin word, *principium*, can mean "principle," "cause," or "beginning."

99. Peter Lombard, *Sententiae* 1. 5, ed. Brady 1: 68.

100. Time could not have existed "in the beginning," because the "beginning" is an indivisible, unextended moment, but for time to exist there must be an extension. If time cannot exist "in the beginning," so the objection runs, then neither can the heavens and the earth, which are temporal creatures.

101. *Liber de causis* §37, ed. Pattin, p. 54; trans. Brand, p. 18.

7. Furthermore, the heavens and the angels were made at the same time, as will be said below.[102] Therefore, the heavens and the earth were not made before all things.

Solution

I answer that holy men have given three different useful interpretations to refute various errors. The first interpretation refutes the error of the Manichees who hold that there are several creative principles, because things are said [according to this first interpretation] to be made by one causal principle, and not by many. Through the second interpretation the error of the eternity of the world is refuted, because the world is held [on this interpretation] to have a beginning of its duration. Through the third interpretation the error is refuted of those holding that the visible things were created by God through the mediation of spiritual creatures, for [on this interpretation] the heavens and the earth are held to have been created first.

Replies to Objections

1. To the first it ought to be said that the designation of being the efficient cause is appropriated to the Father, whereas the designation of being the exemplar cause for a work of art is appropriated to the Son, who is the Wisdom and Art of the Father.[103]

2. To the second it ought to be said that to be "in" as in that which holds and saves, is appropriated to the Holy Spirit, because of the appropriation of goodness, but to be "in," as the artifact is in the skill of the art, and as the thing is in its likeness, is appropriated to the Son.

3. To the third it ought to be said that, according to the opinion that all things were created simultaneously in their [complete] matter and form, things are said [to exist] in the beginning of the time that measures the motion of the first mobile being. Such time does not measure creation but is a by-product of creation, because the creation of things is simultaneous with the beginning of time. According to another opinion, however, which holds that things have been formed over a period of time, ["in the beginning of time"] is not understood

102. Aquinas, *In Sent.* 2.2.2.3.
103. Certain designations are "appropriated" to the various Persons of the Trinity. This means that, whereas the designations are, really, shared by all three Persons, they are thought to be more expressive of the activity of one Person rather than of the other two.

with respect to the time that measures motion or is the number of motion, but with respect to the time which marks the alternation by which the being of the world succeeds the non-being of the world. Or, some others take "time" to mean an "eviternity,"[104] which was created simultaneously with the heavens and the earth.

4. To the fourth it ought to be said that just as number is not numbered by some other number, so time is not measured by some other time, nor is its coming-to-be, since its entire being is its coming-to-be. Hence, time begins at its beginning, not in that which is the measure of time, but in that from which its production begins, as, for example, an animal begins [to grow] from its heart,[105] and a house [begins to be built] from its foundation, and a line [begins to be drawn] from its point.

5. To the fifth it ought to be said that the Philosopher is speaking about the order of nature, as "animal" is said to be prior to "man," not about the order of duration, for the being of the heavens and the earth did not precede time itself.

6. To the sixth it ought to be said that, according to one opinion, all things were created at the same time, not in their individual species, but in unformed matter. According to others, however, all things are created at the same time even in their own forms. In this sense, however, some things were created before others, not in duration, but in the order of nature, as in the order of generation the incomplete comes before the complete. More will be said about this below.[106]

7. To the seventh it ought to be said that by "heavens" is understood also the angelic nature, which is said to dwell in the heavens, and by "earth" is understood all generable and corruptible things.

---

104. "Eviternity" is the translation for *aevum*, the term used in Scholastic Latin to designate the sort of duration, not time, that is appropriate to angels.

105. Aquinas, following Aristotelian biology, thought that the animal's heart was the first organ to be formed.

106. Aquinas, *In Sent.* 2.12.1–5.

Appendices

APPENDIX A □ AQUINAS, *SUMMA THEOLOGIAE* 1.45.5[1]
Whether to create belongs to God alone
Objections
It seems that to create does not belong to God alone.
    1. According to the Philosopher, "what is perfect is able to make something like itself" (*Meteor.* 4.3 [380a14]; *De anima* 2.4 [415a26]). But immaterial creatures are more perfect than material creatures, which do make things like themselves. Fire, for example, generates fire, and man generates man. An immaterial substance, therefore, is able to make a substance like itself. An immaterial substance, however, cannot come to be except by creation, since it does not have matter out of which it comes to be. Some creature, therefore, is able to create.
    2. Furthermore, a greater resistance on the part of the thing made requires a greater power on the part of the maker. A contrary, however, offers more resistance than nothing. Therefore, more power is required to make something out of a contrary, which even a creature can do, than to make something out of nothing. A creature, therefore, is even more able to do this [i.e., to create out of nothing].
    3. Furthermore, the power of the maker is proportionate to that which is made. The created being, however, is finite, as was proved above, when the infinity of God was treated [*Summa theologiae* 1.7.2–4.]. Therefore, to produce something created by creation requires only a finite power. To have finite power, however, is not contrary to a creature's nature. It is not, therefore, impossible for a creature to create.

On the Contrary
    Augustine says, in *On the Trinity* bk. 3, ch. 8,[2] that "neither the good nor the evil angels are able to be the Creators of any thing." Other creatures, therefore, are even less [able to create].

---

    1. For the Latin text, see Aquinas, *Summa theologiae*, 5 vols. (Ottawa: Institutum Studiorum Mediaevalium Ottaviensis, 1941-1945), 1: 287b–289a.
    2. *De trinitate* 3.8 (PL 42: 876; CCL 50: 141); *The Trinity*, trans. Stephen McKenna, (Washington, DC: Catholic University of America Press, 1963), p. 109.

Solution

I answer that, in accord with what has already been said, it is clear enough at first glance that to create can only be the proper action of God alone. More universal effects must be caused by more universal and prior causes. Among all effects, the most universal is being itself. Hence, it must be the proper effect of the first and most universal cause, which is God. Hence, also, it is said in the *Book of Causes*[3] that neither an intelligence nor a "noble soul" gives being, except insofar as it operates with the divine operation. Giving being absolutely, not making this or that being, is what creation means. It is, therefore, clear that creation is the proper action of God Himself.

It is, however, the case that something participates in the proper action of something else, not by its own power but in an instrumental way, as it acts by the power of the other thing. Air, for example, by the power of fire is able to cause both heat and fire. In this way, some have thought that, although creation is the proper action of the universal cause, nevertheless some of the lower causes, acting with the power of the first cause, are able to create. Thus Avicenna has held that the first separated substance created by God creates another [substance] after itself and also a heavenly body and its soul. The heavenly body then creates the matter of the lower bodies. In this way, even the Master [Peter Lombard] says, in bk 2, dist. 4, ch. 3 of the *Sentences,* that God is able to communicate the power of creating to a creature, so that it create as a minister, not on its own authority.

This, however, cannot be, because the secondary instrumental cause participates in the action of the higher cause, only by virtue of that which really belongs to the secondary cause and can be used by the principal cause for its effect. If, therefore, it [a secondary cause] were to act not with what really belongs to itself, it would be used for the action in vain, nor would instruments [then] be properly proportioned to the effects. Thus, for example, we see that a saw, by cutting wood, which [ability] it has from its own form, produces the form of the bench, which is the proper effect of the principal agent. That, however, which is the proper effect of God the Creator is that which is presupposed in all other things, namely, being absolutely. Hence,

---

3. *Liber de causis* §32 (ed. Adriaan Pattin [Louvain: Tijdschrift voor Filosophie, 1966], p. 52); *The Book of Causes,* trans. Dennis J. Brand (Niagara, NY: Niagara University Press, 1981), p. 17.

nothing is able to work toward this effect either by the direction [of another] or as an instrument, since creation presupposes absolutely nothing which could be directed by the action of an instrumental agent. Thus, therefore, it is impossible that some creature create, whether by its own power, or as an instrument, or as a minister. It is especially wrong to say that some bodily thing creates, since no body acts except by touching or moving and, thus, requires in its action something pre-existing that is able to be touched and moved, which is against the meaning of creation.

Replies to Objections

1. To the first it ought to be said that a complete being that participates in its nature[4] makes something like itself, not by producing that nature absolutely but by making that nature come to be in something else. This man, for example, cannot be the cause of human nature absolutely, because he would then be the cause of himself, but he is the cause [as father] of human nature's coming to be in the man whom he generates. He presupposes in his action determined matter, through which a man is an individual. But just as this [individual] man participates in human nature, so any created being participates, so to speak, in the nature of being, because God alone is His being, as was said above. No created being, therefore, is able to produce being absolutely but only being in this [individual]. Thus that through which something is this [individual] must always be presupposed in the action by which [a material creature] makes something like itself. In an immaterial substance, however, something through which it is this [individual] cannot be presupposed, because it is this [individual] through its own form, through which it has being, since [immaterial substances] are subsistent forms. An immaterial substance, therefore, is not able to produce the being of another immaterial substance like itself, but it is able to produce some additional perfection. For example, we might say that a superior angel illuminates a lower angel, as Dionysius says. In this way there is a kind of fatherhood even among

---

4. It participates in its nature rather than *is* its nature. All creatures participate in their natures; no creature *is* its nature. Only God is His nature. Fido is a dog; he participates in the nature of dog. He is not dogness itself. If a thing were its own nature, rather than merely participating in it, it would be a Platonic Form. This is why Plato spoke of dogs, on the one hand, and of "Dogness Itself," on the other.

the heavenly beings, as is clear from the words of the Apostle, Ephesians [3,15]: "From whom all fatherhood in heaven and on earth is named." From this it is also very clear that no created being is able to cause something else, unless there be something presupposed, which is contrary to the meaning of creation.

2. To the second it ought to be said that something comes to be from contraries "accidentally," as is said in the *Physics* 1.7 (190b27). Essentially, however, something comes to be from a subject which is in potency. A contrary, therefore, resists an agent insofar as it blocks the potency from the actuality to which the agent intends to bring the matter. Fire, for example, intends to bring water into the actuality which is similar to itself, but it is blocked by the form and contrary dispositions by which the potency is as it were bound from being brought into actuality. To the extent that the potency is more bound, to that extent a greater power is required in the agent to bring the matter into actuality. Hence a greater power is required in the agent if no potency pre-exists. It is thus, therefore, clear that a much greater power is required to make something out of nothing than to make something out of a contrary.

3. To the third it ought to be said that the power of the maker is measured not only relative to the substance of the thing made but also to the way in which it is made. For example, a greater heat [source] produces not only more heat but does so more quickly. Thus, although to create a finite effect does not require an infinite power, to create it out of nothing does require an infinite power. This is clear from what was said before. Now if the power of the agent must be greater as the potency is farther away from actuality, the power of the agent which presupposes no potency, which is the creative power, must be infinite. [This is so] because there is no comparison between *no* potency and *some* potency, which is presupposed by the power of the natural agent, just as [there is no comparison] between non-being and being. Since no creature has absolutely infinite power, nor infinite being, as was proved above, it follows that no creature is able to create [*Summa theologiae* 1.7.2].

APPENDIX B ☐ AQUINAS, *ON THE ETERNITY OF THE WORLD*[5]

Although we accept according to the Catholic faith that the world had a beginning of its duration, nevertheless the problem has arisen of whether it could have always existed. In order that the truth of this problem be explained, first we must distinguish that about which we agree with our adversaries from that about which we differ from them. If, on the one hand, it is thought that something other than God could have always existed in the sense that something could exist but not [be] made by God, this is an abominable error, not only according to the faith but also according to the philosophers, who admit and prove that absolutely nothing would be able to exist unless it were caused by Him who has being in the highest degree and most truly.[6] If, on the other hand, it is thought that something has always existed and still had been caused completely by God, an investigation should be made whether this can be the case.

Now if it is said that this is impossible, this will be said either because God could not make something which always existed, or because, even if God could make it, it could not be made. On the first part, considering God's infinite power, everyone agrees that God could have made something which always existed. It remains, therefore, to see whether it is possible for something to be made which always existed.

Now if it is said that this cannot be, there are only two reasons or two ways to understand why [this cannot be]: either because of a lack of passive potency, or because of a contradiction in terms. In the first way, it could be said [that] before an angel was made, "an angel is not able to be made," because a passive potency did not pre-exist its being, since it was not made out of pre-existing matter. Nevertheless, God was able to make an angel, and He could make it so that the angel came to be, because He has made [the angel] and [the angel] has been made. Understanding the problem in this way, it must absolutely be granted, according to the faith, that something caused cannot always exist, because to hold this would be to hold that a passive potency

---

5. For the Latin text, see Aquinas, *De aeternitate mundi*, in the Leonine *Opera omnia*, vol. 43 [1976], pp. 49–89.

6. The philosophers referred to here all agree that there is a first cause who makes the world in some way. Aquinas had no experience of a philosopher who did not recognize that there is some sort of first cause of the world.

always existed, which is heretical.[7] Nevertheless it still does not follow from this that God could not make something which always exists.

In the second way, it is said that something cannot be made because of a logical inconsistency, as that it cannot be the case that an affirmation and a negation be simultaneously true, although some say that God could make this so. Others, however, say that not even God can make this so because in fact it is nothing. It is, finally, clear that God cannot make it to be the case [that an affirmation and a negation be simultaneously true], because the very affirmation by which this is held to be so implies its own denial. Still, if it should be held that God is able to make it that things of this sort come to be, the position is not heretical, although I do believe that it is false, just as [to say] that the past has not been includes in itself a contradiction. Augustine, accordingly, in his book *Against Faustus*, [says], "Whoever says this, 'if God is omnipotent, He could make those things which have been made not to have been made,' does not see that this means, 'if God is omnipotent, He could make those things which are true, by the very fact that they are true, to be false.'"[8] Nevertheless, some great men have said piously that God is able to make of the past that it was not the past, and it has not been considered heretical.

It remains, therefore, to be seen whether there is a contradiction between these two ideas, that something is created by God and that it, nevertheless, always existed. Whatever is true in this matter, it will not be heretical to say that God is able to make it to be the case that something created by God always existed. I do believe, however, that

7. "To hold that a passive potency always existed" would be heretical because it would be to hold that there was something other than God that was not created by God. A pre-existent passive potency would exist before creation; hence such a passive potency would be uncreated. Aquinas knew from the decree of the Fourth Lateran Council [1215, "Firmiter credimus ..."] that God is the "Creator of all things, visible and invisible, spiritual and corporal" and that He created both sorts of creatures "at the beginning of time" and "out of nothing" (*Enchiridion symbolorum*, ed. Heinric Denzinger [Freiburg: Herder, 1932], §428). See also James Weisheipl, "The Date and Context of Aquinas' *De aeternitate mundi*," in *Graceful Reason: Essays in Ancient and Medieval Philosophy Presented to Joseph Owens*, ed. Lloyd Gerson (Toronto: Pontifical Institute of Mediaeval Studies, 1983), pp. 239–271, at p. 253.

8. Augustine, *Contra Faustum Manicheum* 26.5 (PL 42: 481; CSEL 25.1: 732); cf. "Reply to Faustus the Manichean," trans. Richard Stothert, in *The Nicene and Post-Nicene Fathers* [first series] ed. Philip Schaff, 14 vols. (New York: Christian Literature Company, 1886–1940), 4: 151–365, at p. 322.

if there were a contradiction, it would be false [to say that God is able to create something that always existed], but if there is no contradiction, it is not only not false but also [not] impossible. It would be erroneous to speak otherwise. Since it is characteristic of the omnipotence of God that it exceed all understanding and power, whoever says that some creature can be thought of that is not able to be made by God expressly derogates from the omnipotence of God. The example of sins is not to the point, because as such they are nothing.[9] In this, therefore, is the entire question: whether to have been absolutely created by God and not to have a beginning of duration are mutually inconsistent or not.

That they are not mutually inconsistent is shown as follows. If they should be inconsistent, this could only be because of one of two reasons or both: (1) either because the efficient cause must precede [its effect] in duration, (2) or because the fact that the creature is said to be made out of nothing requires that non-being precede it in duration.

(1) First I shall show that it is not necessary that an efficient cause, such as God, precede its effect in duration, if He Himself had willed [that He not precede His effect]. First, [I argue] as follows. No cause that instantaneously produces its effect precedes its effect necessarily in duration. But God is a cause that produces His effect, not through motion, but instantaneously. Therefore, it is not necessary that He precede His effect in duration. The first [premise] is clear through induction in all instantaneous changes, like illumination[10] and things of this sort, but nevertheless it is able to be proved through reason as follows.

At whatever moment a thing is assumed to exist, its action can be assumed to begin, as is clear in all generable things, because in the very moment in which fire begins to be it causes heat. But in an instantaneous operation the beginning and the end of it are simul-

9. A sin seems to be a counter example, because it is something that can be thought of but that God cannot do. The sinful feature of an act, however, is a *lack* of moral order rather than something that really exists. Any action just in itself is something positive, something that can and does really exist. The moral quality of the act, however, is something beyond the act in that it concerns the *relation* of the act to an order of goodness. A good action has the quality of moral goodness, but a bad action lacks this quality.

10. That is, as soon as there is light there is illumination; the latter is an effect of the former. Aquinas *also* thinks that light travels distances instantaneously.

taneous, or rather, are identical. At whatever moment, therefore, the agent is assumed to produce its effect instantaneously, the end of its action can be assumed to exist. But the end of action is simultaneous with the completed thing. Therefore, it is not inconsistent if the cause producing its effect instantaneously does not precede its effect in duration. It is inconsistent, however, in causes that produce their effects through motion, because the beginning of motion must precede the end of it. And because men are accustomed to consider productions [of things] that involve motion, they do not, therefore, easily grasp that the efficient cause does not [necessarily] precede its effect in duration. So it is that those with little experience and but superficial observations are the quickest to make pronouncements.

The fact that God is an efficient cause through will cannot weaken the force of this argument, because it is not necessary that even a will precede its effect in duration, and an agent through will only [precedes its effect in duration] when it acts from deliberation, which we should never attribute to God.[11]

Furthermore, a cause which produces the entire substance of a thing does not accomplish less in producing the entire substance than a cause which produces the form [accomplishes] in producing a form. On the contrary, it [accomplishes] much more, because it produces not by working from the potency of matter, as does that which produces the form. But some agents which produce the form alone are able to produce the form whenever they exist, as is clear when the sun is illuminating. Therefore, even more, God, who produces the entire substance of a thing, is able to make His effect exist whenever He exists.

Furthermore, if there is a cause the effect of which does not exist at the very same time that the cause exists, this can only happen because something is lacking to the cause that would make it complete, because a complete cause and its effect are simultaneous. There is, however, never anything lacking [which is needed] to complete God. Therefore, as long as God is taken to exist, His effect can be taken to exist, and it is thus not necessary that He precede [His effect] in duration.

11. God does not *deliberate* in making a decision, that is, He does not go through a successive process of reviewing, one by one, reasons for a decision. God's mind does not understand through a temporal, successive process of reasoning, as the human mind does, and hence there is no deliberation in God's mind.

Furthermore, the will of one who has a will does not diminish his power, and this is certainly true of God. But all those who take issue with Aristotle's arguments by which it is proved that things [caused] by God have always existed because what is always the same always does the same, say that this would follow if He were not an agent through will. Therefore, even if He is taken to be an agent through will, it follows that He is able to make it the case that something caused by Him always exists. And thus it is clear that it is not inconsistent to say that the agent does not precede its effect in duration, because God is [only] not able to do those things that are logically inconsistent.

(2) Now it remains to be seen whether it is inconsistent that something made has always existed because, since it is said to have been made out of nothing, its non-being must necessarily precede it in duration. That there is no inconsistency is shown by what Anselm has said in his *Monologion*, chapter 8, where he explains how the creature is said to have been made out of nothing. "The third meaning," he says, "according to which something is said to have been made out of nothing is [that by which] we mean that something has really been made but there is not something from which it has been made. Similarly, when a man is said to have been saddened for no reason, he is said, it seems, to be saddened from nothing. It will not be inconsistent, therefore, if what has been concluded is understood according to this meaning, that other than the highest essence all things which are have been made from nothing, that is, not from something."[12] Hence it is clear according to this explanation that no order is supposed between what has been made and nothing, as though what has been made would have to have been nothing [first] and later be something.

Furthermore, let it be supposed that the order to nothing implied in the preposition ["out of"] remains affirmed, so that the sense is, the creature has been made out of nothing, that is, has been made after nothing. This word "after" implies order absolutely. There are, however, several kinds of order, such as that of duration and that of nature. If the proper and the particular is not implied by the common and the

12. Anselm, *Monologion* §8, in *Opera Omnia*, ed. Francis S. Schmitt, 6 vols. (Edinburgh: Thomas Nelson, 1938–1961), 1: 23; cf. *Anselm of Canterbury*, trans. Jasper Hopkins and Herbert W. Richardson, 4 vols. (Toronto and New York: Edwin Mellen Press, 1974–1976), 1: 17.

universal, it would not be necessary that nothing precede *in duration* that which comes later, just because the creature is said to be *after* nothing, but it is enough that nothing be prior *by nature* to being. What is naturally prior in every thing is what belongs to itself rather than what it has only from another. Now a creature has no being except [what it has] from another, and if it is left to itself it is nothing. Hence nothing [itself] in the creature is naturally prior to being. And this does not imply that nothing and being are simultaneous because [nothing] does not precede [being] in duration. If the creature has always existed, it is not supposed that at some time it was nothing, but rather it is supposed that its nature is such that it would be nothing if it were left to itself. For example, if we should say that air has always been illuminated by the sun, it will be right to say that the air has been made light by the sun. Since whatever comes to be comes to be from an incompatible, that is, from what cannot compatibly exist at the same time with that which is said to have come to be, it will be right to say that what has been made light [has been made so] from the non-light or from the dark – not that it would ever have been not light or dark, but that it would be such if the sun left it to itself. This is very clear in stars and heavenly bodies that are always illuminated by the sun.

It is thus, therefore, clear that to say that something has been made by God and that it has always existed is not a contradiction. If there were a contradiction, it is a wonder that Augustine did not see it, because this would have been the strongest way of disproving the eternity of the world. Nevertheless, when he argued against the eternity of the world with many arguments in books 11 and 12 of *The City of God*, he completely omitted this way. On the contrary, he seems to suggest that there is no contradiction, for he says in book 10, *The City of God*, chapter 31, speaking about the Platonists, "They have come up with their understanding of this, that there is not a beginning of time but [only] of dependence. They say, for example, that if a foot had existed from eternity in dust, there would always have been a footprint there, but nevertheless no one would doubt that the footprint had been made by the person putting his foot down. And one is not prior to the other, although one was made by the other. Thus, they say, both the world and the gods created in it have always existed, provided that he who made them always exists, and nevertheless they have been made." And Augustine never says that this is a contradiction, but he argues against them in another way. He also says in book 11, chapter 4, "Those who claim that the world has been made by God but do not grant it a beginning of time but only a beginning in the sense that it was created, so that, in a sense that can hardly be understood, the world was always made, do say something sensible." The reason it can "hardly be understood" is given in the first argument.[13]

It is also a wonder that the most noble of philosophers have not noticed this [alleged] inconsistency. Indeed, Augustine says in the same book, chapter 5, speaking against those about whom mention was made in the previous text, "We are dealing with those who agree with us that God is the Creator of all bodies and of all natures which are not Himself."[14] He later added about them, "These have surpassed other philosophers in nobility and authority." This same thing will also appear to anyone who carefully considers what has been said by those who think the world has always existed and nevertheless has been made by God, and who see no contradiction in this. Those, therefore, who have so subtly seen the inconsistency are the only ones [who have done so], and with them [so they might think] arises all wisdom!

Nevertheless, because some authorities seem to agree with them, it ought to be shown that [such authorities] provide very weak support for them. Damascene, for example, says in book 1, chapter 8, "It is not naturally suitable that what is brought from non-being to being be co-eternal with that which is without beginning and is always."[15] Also, Hugh of Saint Victor, in the beginning of his book *On the Sacraments*, says, "the power of the ineffable omnipotence does not allow anything to be co-eternal with Himself, so that He would be helped in His own activity."[16]

13. Augustine, *De civitate Dei* 10.31 (PL 41: 311; CCL 47: 309) and 11.4 (PL 41: 319; CCL 48: 324); cf. *The City of God*, trans. Henry Bettenson (Harmondsworth, UK: Penguin, 1961), pp. 420 and 432–433. See also above, pp. 116–118.

14. *De civitate Dei* 10.5 (PL 41: 319–320; CCL 48: 325); trans. Bettenson, p. 434.

15. John Damascene *De fide orthodoxa* 1.8 (PG 94: 814b); ed. Eligius M. Buytaert (St. Bonaventure, NY: Franciscan Institute, 1955), p. 32; cf. "The Orthodox Faith," trans. Frederic H. Chase, in Saint John of Damascus, *Writings* (New York: Fathers of the Church, 1958), p. 179.

16. Hugh of St. Victor, *De sacramentis* 1.1 (PL 176: 187b); cf. *Hugh of St. Victor on the Sacraments of the Faith*, trans. Roy J. Deferrari (Cambridge, MA: Medieval Academy of America, 1951), pp. 5–6.

The way, however, to understand these and similar authorities is clear in what Boethius says in the last book of *The Consolation of Philosophy*: "When some hear that the world was not understood by Plato to have had a beginning of time and not to have an end in the future, they do not rightly judge [when they conclude] that the world has been built in this way to be co-eternal with the builder. Indeed, it is one thing to have an unending life, which Plato attributes to the world, but it is another to have the entire presence of an unending life all at once, which is clearly the property of the Divine Mind."[17] It is hence clear also that the objection of some people does not follow, namely, that the creature [even if always existing] would be equal to God in duration.

That it may thus be said that nothing can be in any way co-eternal with God, because nothing is immutable except God alone, is clear by what Augustine says in book 12, *The City of God*, chapter 16. "Since time is always flowing it cannot be co-eternal with the immutable eternity. Hence, even if the immortality of angels does not run in time, nor is their past as though no longer existent, nor their future as though not yet existent, still their actions, by which times are marked, run from what will be into what has been. Hence they are not able to be co-eternal with the Creator, in whose action it cannot be said that what was is not any longer, or that what will be is not yet." Likewise also he says in book 8, *On the Literal Meaning of Genesis*, "Because the nature of the Trinity is completely unchangeable, it is therefore eternal such that something can not be co-eternal with it." He says something similar in the 11th book of the *Confessions*.[18]

[Some objectors] also add arguments on their own, which the philosophers touch upon and answer, among which the most difficult is that about the infinity of souls. If the world always existed, it is necessary that now there are an infinite number of souls. But this argument is not germane, because God could have made a world without

17. Boethius, *De consolatione philosophiae* 5.6 (PL 63: 859b; CCL 94: 101); cf. "The Consolation of Philosophy," trans. S.J. Tester, in *Boethius*, 2nd ed. (Cambridge, MA: Harvard University Press; London: Heinemann, 1973), pp. 424–425.

18. The references to Augustine, are to: *De civitate Dei* 12.16 (PL 41: 364–365; CCL 48: 372), trans. Bettenson, pp. 490–491; *De Genesi ad litteram* 8.23 (PL 34: 389; CSEL 28.1: 262), cf. *The Literal Meaning of Genesis*, trans. John Taylor, 2 vols. (New York: Newman Press, 1982), 1: 63; and *Confessiones* 11.30 (PL 32: 826; CCL 27: 215), cf. *Confessions*, trans. R.S. Pine-Coffin (Harmondsworth: Penguin, 1961), p. 279.

men and without souls and without animals, or He could have made men to be when in fact He did make them, even if He had made the whole world from eternity. Thus there would not remain an infinite number of souls after [the death of] bodies. Furthermore, it has not yet been demonstrated that God could not make an actual infinity of things [... *non est adhuc demonstratum quod Deus non possit facere ut sint infinita actu*].

I omit for the present a response to other arguments, both because I have responded to them elsewhere and because some of them are so weak that, by their weakness, they seem to give plausibility to the other side of the debate.

APPENDIX C ☐ AQUINAS, *COMMENTARY ON ARISTOTLE'S PHYSICS* [selections][19]
Book 8, Lecture 2
[976] Aristotle argues as follows for the eternity of motion.] If motion has not always existed, one must say either that movers and the things moved were made at some time, before which they did not exist, or that they are eternal. If it should be said that every movable object has been made, one must say that before the first change there was another change and a motion, by which the mobile thing itself was made. The reasoning for this depends upon what has been said. If it is granted that motion has not been eternal, but that there is some first change before which there was no change, it will follow that that first change involved some movable object, and that the movable object was made because it did not exist before, since all movable objects are considered to have been made. Whatever comes to be which was not in existence before comes to be through some motion or change. The motion or change through which the movable object comes into being is prior to the change by which the movable object is moved. Therefore, before the change which is supposed to be first there is another change, and so on infinitely ... .

If it is granted that there are movable objects and movers and that at some time the first mover begins to move something which was

19. For the Latin text, see Aquinas, *Expositio in octos libros Physicorum Aristotelis* 8.2, ed. P.M. Maggiolo (Turin: Marietti, 1965), §§976, 982–983, 986–990; cf. *Commentary on Aristotle's "Physics,"* trans. Richard J. Blackwell et al. (New Haven, CT: Yale University Press, 1963), pp. 474–487.

resting and not moving before, we must say that there is another change made in the mover or in the movable object before the first mover began to move. This is clear as follows. Rest is the privation of motion. Privation, however, is not in that which is receptive of a habit or of a form except through some cause. There was, therefore, some cause either on the part of the mover or on the part of the movable object which was the cause of the rest. The state of rest remained, therefore, as long as the cause endured. If, therefore, at some time the mover begins to move, this cause of rest must be removed. It cannot be removed, however, except through some motion or change. It follows, therefore, that before the change which was said to be first, there was another earlier change by which the cause of rest was removed.

[982] Aristotle advances a supporting argument from time.] It is impossible to say or to think that there is time without the present moment, just as it is impossible for a line to exist without a point. Moreover, the present moment is an intermediate of sorts, having the nature of being both a beginning and an end, that is, the beginning of the future and the end of the past. From this it seems that time must be eternal, for whatever time is taken, its limit on either side is a moment. This is clear because no part of time is actual except the present moment. What has passed has already gone, and what is future is not yet. The moment, however, which is taken as the limit of time is both a beginning and an end, as was said. Therefore, on either side of any given time there must always be time. Otherwise, the first moment would not be an end, and the last moment would not be a beginning. From the statement that time is eternal, [Aristotle] concludes that motion must be eternal, because time is a property of motion insofar as it is the number of motion, as was said.

[983] It seems, however, that Aristotle's argument is not sound. For the present moment is related to time just as a point is related to a line, as was said in the sixth book [of the *Physics*]. It is not, however, in the nature of a point that it be an intermediary. Indeed, in a line, one point is only the beginning, and another is only the end. If it were the case that *every* point were a beginning and an end, then the line would have to be infinite. It could not, therefore, be proven that a line is infinite from the claim that every point is a beginning and an end. It would be, rather, the other way around: from the given that a line is infinite, it could be proved that every point was a beginning and an end. Simi-

larly, the claim that every moment is a beginning and an end is only true if time is supposed to be eternal. In the assumption of this intermediate [nature of any moment], therefore, Aristotle seems to be supposing the eternity of time, which is what he ought to be proving ... .

[986] These then are arguments by which Aristotle intends to prove that motion always existed and never ceases. One part of his position conflicts with our faith, namely, [Aristotle's position] that motion always existed. According to our faith, nothing is supposed to have always existed except God alone, who is completely immovable, unless someone should wish to call the divine act of understanding a kind of motion, although that would be to understand it equivocally. Aristotle does not intend such motion, but rather motion in the proper sense of the word.

The other part of his position, however, is not completely contrary to the faith, because, as was said above, Aristotle does not deal with the motion of the heavens but with motion in general. We hold, according to our faith, that the substance of the world at some time has begun to exist but that, nevertheless, it should not cease to exist. We also hold that some motions will always exist, especially those in men, who will always remain, living an incorruptible life, whether of misery of or blessedness.

Some, vainly attempting to show that Aristotle has not spoken against the faith, have said that Aristotle does not intend to prove here, as something true, that motion was eternal, but rather [intends] to give arguments on both sides, as though on a doubtful matter. But this seems foolish, given [Aristotle's] mode of proceeding. And furthermore, the eternity of time and motion is used as a foundation [by Aristotle] to prove that the first principle [God] exists. Both here in the eighth book [of the *Physics*] and in the twelfth book of the *Metaphysics* he clearly supposes this [the eternity of time and motion] as something proven.

[987] But if one correctly considers the arguments given here, it can be seen that the truth of the faith cannot be refuted with arguments of this sort. There are, to be sure, sound arguments of this sort for proving that motion has not begun through natural causes, as is supposed by some. But it cannot be proven with these arguments that motion did not begin from a first principle such that, as our faith holds, all

things were produced anew. This is clear to anyone who considers the individual inferences given here.

If one asks, given that motion has not always existed, whether or not movers and movable things have always existed, the answer should be that the first mover has always existed, but that all other things, whether they are movers or movable things, have not always existed. Rather, the beginning of their existence was caused by the universal cause of all being. It has been shown above that the production of all being from the first cause of being is not a motion, whether this is supposed to have been an eternal emanation of things or not. It does not, therefore, follow that before the first change there was some other change. It would follow, however, if the movers and movable things were brought into being by some limited agent, which would act by transforming a pre-existing subject from non-being to being, or from privation to form. Aristotle's argument concerns this kind of beginning.

[988] But since we suppose that at least the first mover has always existed, an answer should be made to his next argument, namely, that if movers and movable things pre-existed, and if motion begins to be anew, the movers or the movable things could not have been in the same state before as they are when there is motion, and hence there must have been a change before the "first" change.

Now if we should speak about the motion itself, the answer is easy, for the movable things were not in the same state before in which they now are, because before they did not exist. Hence they were not able to be moved. As has been said, they did not receive being itself through a change or a motion, but through an emanation from the first principle of things. Thus it does not follow that before the first change there was another change.

But there still remains the question about the first production of things. If the first principle, which is God, is not in a different state now from before [He produced things], He does not produce things now rather than before. If, on the other hand, He is in a different state, there will be at least a change on His part that will be before the change which is supposed to be first.

Now if He were an agent that acts only through nature, and not through will and intellect, the argument would be necessarily sound. But because He acts through will, He is able through His eternal will to produce a non-eternal effect, just as with His eternal intellect He is able to understand a non-eternal thing. This is so, because the thing understood is, in a certain way, the principle of action in those agents that act through will, just as the natural form [is the principle of action] in those agents that act through nature.

[989] But let us proceed further. We think [so the objection would contend] that a will delays doing what it wishes only because it expects something in the future which is not yet present. For example, I wish to build a fire, not now but later, when I expect the cold, which is the cause of my making the fire; or so I expect at the present. Because, however, time is successive, this [my delaying something] cannot occur without motion. Thus a will, even if it is supposed to be immutable, cannot delay doing what it wishes unless there is some motion intervening. And thus there cannot be a new production of things that comes from an eternal will, unless there should be some intermediary motions that follow that will infinitely.

It escapes the notice of those who object in this way, however, that this objection concerns the temporal agent, which acts in a presupposed time. In an action of the sort that occurs in time, we must recognize a determinate relation to a particular time, or to something that belongs to a particular time, so that the action occurs in one time rather than in another. But this argument is irrelevant to the universal agent, which produces both time itself and all other things.

When we say that things have not always been produced by God, we do not understand that an infinite time preceded, in which God did not act, and after at a determined time He began to act. Rather, God brought into being both time and things together after they had not existed. And hence it is not fitting to think that the divine will wished to make things not then but later, as though there were a lapse of time; rather we should think simply this: that He wished that things and time have a beginning of their duration after they had not existed.

If, moreover, one should ask why He wished it this way, the response should doubtless be that He wished it because of Himself. For just as He made things for Himself, so that a likeness of His goodness might be manifested in them, so He wished that they have not always existed, so that His self-sufficiency be manifested, in that, without the existence of all other things, He Himself has had complete sufficiency of blessedness, and also of power for the production of things.

This, at least, can be said, as far as human reason can grasp the divine, but we must always recognize that the divine wisdom cannot be comprehended by us.

[990. Aquinas responds to Aristotle's arguments concerning the eternity of time.] ... Aristotle's argument that there can be no before and after without time is not sound. When we say that the beginning of time is "before which there is nothing," it does not follow that the moment itself which is the beginning of time be preceded by a time which is signified by saying "before." If, for example, I should say that the beginning of a spatial magnitude is "that outside of which there is nothing of it," it does not follow that "outside of that beginning" signifies some place that exists in reality, but rather [it signifies a place] in the imagination only. Otherwise, we should have to suppose a place outside of the heavens, the magnitude of which is finite, that is, with a beginning and an end. Likewise, no really existing time, but only time in our imagination, precedes the first moment which is the beginning of time. And this time is meant when it is said that the first moment is the beginning of time, "before which" there is nothing of time.

Or, it could be said, when the beginning of time is said to be "before which there is nothing of time," that the "before" is not affirmative but negative. In this way one need not suppose a time before the beginning of time. In temporal matters, something always pre-exists a beginning of time, as when it is said that the beginning of youth is that "before which there is nothing of youth," the "before" remains affirmative, because the period of youth is measured by time. Time, however, is not measured by time. Accordingly, no time precedes its beginning. Thus the "before," which is supposed in the definition of the beginning of time, need not be affirmed but rather negated.

Nevertheless, there is before time a duration, namely, the eternity of God, which has no extension, and no before and after, as does time, but is a simultaneous whole. [The divine duration] cannot be compared with time, just as the divine magnitude cannot be compared with a corporeal magnitude. When we say, therefore, that outside of the world there is nothing but God, we do not mean that there is some [real] dimension outside of the world; in like manner, when we say that before the world nothing existed, we do not mean that there is some successive duration before the world.

APPENDIX D ☐ AQUINAS' ATTRIBUTION OF CREATION TO ARISTOTLE[20]

Aquinas, *Commentary on Aristotle's "Physics"*[21]

Book 8, Lecture 3

[996] Just as some things are always true and nevertheless have a cause of their truth, so Aristotle understood that some beings have always existed, namely, the heavenly bodies and separated substances, and nevertheless have had a cause of their being.

Book 8, Lecture 21

[1154] Everything which is not its own being participates in being from the first cause, which is its own being. Hence, even Averroes in the book, *On the Substance of the World*, admits that God is the cause of the heavens, not only of their motion, but even of their very substance – and this could only be because they have their being from God. Moreover, the only being they have from Him is perpetual being; therefore, they have their perpetuity from another. The words of Aristotle are also in accord with this, because he says in the fifth and eighth books of the *Metaphysics* that certain beings are necessary which have a cause of their necessity. With this being supposed, the solution according to the mind of Alexander is clear, namely, that just as a heavenly body has its being-moved from another, so also it has its being from another. Hence, just as perpetual motion manifests the infinite power of the mover, although not of the movable thing, so also the perpetual duration of it manifests the infinite power of the cause from which it has being.

20. Here, in chronological order, are the texts in which Aquinas attributes a doctrine of creation to Aristotle: *Scriptum super libros Sententiarum* 2.1.1.5, sol. and 2.1, expositio textus (*ca* 1253); *De articulis fidei* (1261–1265); *Quaestiones disputate De potentia Dei* 3. 5 (1265–1266); *Expositio super primam decretalem* (1261–1269); *Expositio in octos libros Physicorum Aristotlis* 8.2.[4–5] and 8.3.[6] (1270–1271); *Expositio in duodecim libros Metaphysicorum Aristotelis* 2.2 and 6.1 (1269–1272); *De substantiis separatis* 9 (1271–1273); *Expositio in libros Aristotelis De caelo et mundo* 1.8 (1272–1273). This list is adapted from Steven E. Baldner, "The Doctrine of St. Thomas Aquinas on the Eternity of the World," unpublished Licentiate Thesis (Toronto: Pontifical Institute of Mediaeval Studies, 1979), pp. 96–100. See also Mark Johnson, "Did St. Thomas Attribute a Doctrine of Creation to Aristotle?" *The New Scholasticism* 63 (1989): 129–155.

21. For the Latin text, see Aquinas, *Expositio in octos libros Physicorum* 8.3, 21, ed. Maggiolo §§996, 1154; trans. Blackwell et al., pp. 490, 581.

Aquinas, *On Separated Substances* **9**[22]
It ought not to be thought that Plato and Aristotle, because they supposed that immaterial substances or even heavenly bodies have always existed, denied that such things had a cause of existing. For they do not deviate from the position of the Catholic faith because they have supposed these things to be uncreated but because they have supposed them to have always existed.

APPENDIX E ☐ AQUINAS, *WRITINGS ON THE SENTENCES OF PETER LOMBARD*[23]
Book 2, Prologue
> "His spirit has decorated the heavens and by His mid-
> wife's hand the twisted snake has been brought forth."
> Job [26:13]

Both theologians and philosophers consider creatures, but they do so in different ways. Philosophers consider creatures as they exist in their own proper natures; hence, they investigate the proper causes and attributes of things. The theologian, however, considers creatures as they come from the first principle and as they are ordered to their ultimate end, both of which are God. Theology, therefore, is rightly called divine wisdom, because it considers the highest cause, which is God. It is fittingly said in Ecclesiasticus [or the Book of Sirach, 42:17], "Has not the Lord made his saints to tell all His marvelous deeds?" In this Second Book [of the *Sentences*], creatures are discussed in the theological way. In the verse given above [from Job], three major topics for our subject can be noticed, namely, the *principle* of things, the *act* of this principle, and the *effect* of this act.

On the part of the *principle* two things are touched upon, namely, "spirit" and "hand": the spirit of goodness or of God's will, and the hand of power. Concerning this spirit it is said in Psalm [103:30], "Send

22. For the Latin text, see Aquinas, *De substantiis separatiis,* ed. H.-F. Dondaine, in the Leonine *Opera omnia,* vol. 40 [1969], p. D58; cf. *Treatise on Separate Substances,* trans. Francis J. Lescoe (West Hartford, CT: St. Joseph College, 1965), p. 63.
23. For the Latin text, see Aquinas, *Scriptum super libros Sententiarum Petri Lombardi,* ed. P. Mandonnet and M.F. Moos, 4 vols. (Paris: P. Lethielleux, 1929–1947), 2: 1–3.

forth your Spirit and they will be created." According to Dionysius, *On the Divine Names*, chapter 4,[24] just as the sun sends forth its rays for illuminating bodies, so the Divine Goodness pours forth its rays, that is, its causality, for the creation of things. And in the same way Augustine, *On Christian Doctrine*, book 1, chapter 32,[25] says that insofar as God is good we exist. The ones who have denied this spirit are those who have held that God had produced things out of the necessity of nature and not from the freedom of the will. Against these Dionysius, *On the Divine Names*, chapter 4,[26] says that Divine Love has not allowed itself to be without fruit.

Concerning the "hand" of His power, this is said in Psalm [103:28], "When you opened your hand, all things were filled with goodness." To be sure, in His hand were all the ends of the earth, because nothing existed from all eternity except by His power. When the hand has been opened, by the key of love, the creatures have come forth. This is the hand about which Isaiah [59:1] says, "Behold, the Lord's hand has not been shortened," because He produces the substance of things into being by His infinite power. Those who have taught that God is not able to make something to exist from nothing have wished "to shorten" this hand.

And thus the Trinity of Persons appears in the production of creatures. "Spirit" indicates the Holy Spirit, about whom it is said in the Book of Wisdom [1:7], "The Spirit of the Lord has filled the whole earth." "Hand" indicates the Son, who is also called the arm of the Father [Job 40:4], "Do you have an arm like God's and do you thunder with a voice like God's?" because He is the power and the wisdom of God. The pronoun "Him" in "All things have been made through Him" [John 1:3] refers to the Father, but the Son and the Holy Spirit are also indicated, about whom it is said in Genesis [1:1], "In the beginning God created the heavens and the earth."

24. Dionysius Areopagite, *De divinis nominibus* 4.1 (PG 3: 693b), ed. Beate Regina Suchla, in Corpus Dionysiacum 1 (Berlin and New York: Walter de Gruyter, 1990), pp. 143–144; cf. *The Divine Names and Mystical Theology*, trans. John D. Jones (Milwaukee, WI: Marquette University Press, 1980), p. 133.

25. Augustine, *De doctrina christiana* 1.32 (CCSL 32: 26.3–4); cf. *On Christian Doctrine*, trans. D.W. Robertson (Indianapolis, IN: Bobbs-Merrill, 1958), p. 27.

26. Dionysius, *De divinis nominibus* 4.10 (PG 3: 708a), ed. Suchla, p. 155; trans. Jones, p. 143.

On the part of *act* Job touches on two things: the "decoration" and the role of the "mid-wife". Decoration pertains to the ordering of things, because God has decorated them with different kinds of beauty. As is said in Ecclesiasticus [42:21], "The Lord has decorated the great works of his wisdom." Boethius (*On the Consolation of Philosophy*, book 3, meter 9) says about this beauty: "[You being] most beautiful produce the beautiful world by your mind."²⁷ Mid-wifery pertains to the governing of providence, by which, since creatures are not able to subsist by themselves, God, like a mid-wife, conserves them in being, provides what is needful for their end, and drives away what is harmful, even using evil to further good ends. Whence it is said in Job [38:8], with a similar metaphor, "Who has closed the sea with doors when it burst forth as though coming from the womb?"

On the part of *effect*, Job touches two things, namely, "the heavens" and the "twisted snake." About the heavens we are able to consider two things, *firmness*, as in Proverbs [3:19], "His wisdom has made the heavens firm," and *unending luminosity*, about which it is said [Ecclesiasticus 24:6], "I have made to rise in the heavens a light that will not fail." Hence by "heavens" we can understand creatures which will persist firmly in their own beauty.

Likewise by "twisted snake" we can consider two things, namely, darkness and crookedness. The first is indicated in the name of "snake" [*coluber*], because "snake" indicates "abiding in the shades" [*coluber = colens umbram*], which signifies the lack of light. Crookedness is indicated by "twisted", for what is twisted (or distorted) is bent from rightness. Hence, by "twisted snake" those creatures can be understood of whom the beauty and rightness have been darkened by sin. The Devil is chiefly meant, "by whose envy death has entered into the world," [Wisdom 2:24], about whose darkness it is said [Job 40:16], "he sleeps in the shade, in the hidden place beneath the reed," and about whose twistedness it is said [Isaiah 27:1] "The Lord will bring down his sword, hard, great, and fearful, upon the Leviathan, the swift serpent, and He shall kill the twisted serpent."

Rightly, therefore, God is said to have decorated the heavens, because he has kept creatures in their order and the divine goodness shines forth clearly and the decoration of beauty has not been lost.

27. Boethius, *De consolatione philosophiae* 3.m9 (PL 63: 758–759; CCL 94: 51–52); trans. Tester, pp. 272–273.

Rightly also the twisted snake is said to have been brought forth by the mid-wife's hand, because the divine power shines forth even among the wicked in the fact that they are held back, and the divine providence shines forth through the fact that their evil deeds are turned into good. And so the material of this Second Book [of the *Sentences*] is manifest, in which is treated the making of creatures and the fall through sin of the angel and of man.

Glossary

This glossary contains some important terms used in Aquinas' *Writings on the Sentences*, especially the section translated above (2.1.1).

accident: see *substance* and *accident*

act, actual, or *actuality; potency, potential,* or *potentiality.*
That which is, is "actual." That which can be, but is not, is "potential." For example, the boiling water is actually hot, but is potentially cold. A man with little money is, in actuality, poor, but, in potentiality, he is rich, for he may win the lottery. The flowers are growing now in act, but in potency they are nutrients in the soil. All things that we experience in this material world are both actual and potential: they actually are whatever they are, but they are potentially something else, for they may change. The fact that all such things are both actual and potential means that all things are composed of two different principles: *form,* the principle of actuality, and *matter,* the principle of potentiality.

active potency and *passive potency*
Potency, in general, indicates what can be, but this can be understood in two different ways. Actively, a thing may have a potency because it is able to perform some operation or activity. A normal adult has the active potency to learn the Gaelic language; such a person has the ability or the power to learn the language. So an active potency can be understood to be a power or an ability, which may or may not be put to use. A passive potency, on the other hand, is a characteristic a thing has to have something done to it. A pile of lumber could be built into a work bench; a compound could be changed into its elements; the ham in the refrigerator could be turned into human substance.

alteration: see *change*

angel, separated substance, intelligence, separate intelligence
These terms have different meanings, but they have a meaning in common. They all can be used to indicate a substance that has no matter; such a being would be a pure substantial form that exists without matter. Its activity would be primarily the activity of

knowing, and hence it is often referred to as an intelligence or a separate intelligence. The term "separated" or "separate" indicates separate from matter.

appropriation

This term is used to express the fact that a certain operation is associated more with one Person of the Trinity than with others, even though the operation in question is really performed by the Godhead as a whole. The work of creation, for example, is said to be appropriated to the Father, even though the work of creation is the work of the entire Trinity.

categories of being

There are ten basic categories of being, the category of substance and nine categories of accidents. These categories are the basic terms in which all things can be defined. As the basic terms of all definitions, they are not themselves definable. The nine categories of accidents are: quantity, quality, relation, being active, being passive, when, where, position, and possessing. See also *substance* and *accident*.

cause and *effect*; *causality*; see also *principle*

A cause is that upon which something else, its effect, depends for its being or for its coming to be. When we ask the question "why?" the answer that we are looking for is a cause. There are four main kinds of causes.

1. *efficient cause*. This is the cause that produces something, makes something, moves something. It is the answer to the question, "who or what caused or made this?" Synonym: *agent*. The carpenter who builds the house, the heat that evaporates the water, and the rock that produces the ripples in the pond are all examples of efficient causes.

2. *final cause*. The goal or end of some process or activity. It is the answer to the question, "for what reason is this done?" A man eats because he is hungry; birds have hollow bones in order to be light in weight for flight; beavers build dams to supply themselves with water for the protection of their lodges; and an acorn grows in order to become an oak tree. These are all examples of final causes.

3. *formal cause*. The form, intelligible structure, act, actuality of some thing. See *act*; *form*. The formal cause is an intrinsic principle of a thing that makes it to be what it is. It is the answer to the

question, "what is it?" The shape of a table, the atomic structure of a molecule, the definition of any natural thing are all examples of formal causality.

4. *material cause*. The matter, the stuff, the passive potency, the potentiality, the materials. See *act* and *potency*; *form* and *matter*. The material cause is the intrinsic principle that allows a thing to be changed into something other than it is. It is the answer to the question, "out of what is the thing made?" The lumber out of which the table is made, the hydrogen and oxygen of water, and the chemicals of a living thing are all examples of material causes.

change and *motion*

These terms are used synonymously. Change or motion really exists, but as it is not a fixed thing it is very hard to define. The best definition is given in terms of actuality and potentiality: motion is the actuality of something in potentiality while it is in potentiality. Motion is neither actuality alone, for then the motion would be over and done with, nor is it potentiality alone, for then the motion would not yet have occurred; hence the awkward but really accurate definition given above. The motion of an arrow shot from a bow, for example, is the actuality of the potentiality of the arrow to strike the target as a realized potentiality (and thus the arrow is no longer in the bow nor as yet has reached the target). There are four main kinds of change or motion.

1. *local motion*. This is motion from one place to another place.

2. *alteration*. This is the change in a quality, as when something changes color.

3. *increase* or *augmentation* and *decrease*. This is a change in the quantity of a thing as when a thing grows or expands.

4. *generation* and *corruption*. This is the most radical sort of change; it is not in the strict sense a motion, for it occurs instantaneously, but in the broad sense it is a kind of change. Generation is the coming into being of a substance, as when a chemical compound comes into being from its elements or when an animal comes into being from the seed and egg of the parents. Corruption, on the other hand, is the going out of being of a substance, as when a compound is reduced to its elements or when an animal dies. Corruption here is not used in a moral sense. See also *corruptible* and *incorruptible*.

contraries and *privatives*

These terms are used to express different ways in which two things may be opposed to one another, that is, two ways in which one thing is the contradictory of another. A privative is the lack of something that can or should be present in something. Thus, blindness is the privative of sight, evil is the privative of good. A contrary is the opposite end of a scale from another contrary. Thus, the color black is the contrary of the color white, for there are many colors in between, and hot is the contrary of cold, for there are degrees of heat and cold inbetween the two.

corruptible and *incorruptible*

That which is corruptible is liable to generation and corruption; that is, it is a substance that can be made out of something and can cease to exist by decaying into its constituent elements. All material things are, thus, corruptible, for they are all made out of something and they will all decay into the elements out of which they were made. An incorruptible substance, on the other hand, is one that is not made out of anything and that, therefore, cannot decay into its elements. Spiritual substances (angels, human souls), are incorruptible.

demonstration

An argument that produces true scientific knowledge. It shows how something is true and how it cannot be other than it is. It is an argument in the strongest sense of the term. Contrast this with a *probable* or *dialectical* argument, which produces not knowledge but opinion. A probable argument may produce a very reasonable conclusion, but it may yet be a conclusion that someone could reasonably have some doubts about. No reasonable person, however, could doubt the conclusion of a demonstration. A *sophistical* argument, finally, is no argument at all, but the mere appearance of an argument. It is faulty or deceptive reasoning.

dialectical argument: see *demonstration*

effect: see *cause*

efficient cause: see *cause*

emanation

Emanation is a term used to designate a doctrine that God is the ultimate cause of the existence of all things. In this general sense, emanation is like creation. Emanation, however, can differ from creation in at least one of three ways. 1) Emanation can mean that God makes things, not out of nothing, but out of Himself. In this sense, the creatures are not really independently existing beings but are extensions of God's being. 2) Emanation can mean that God creates out of nothing but creates only one creature immediately; all other creatures are created through the intermediate causality of the first and of some subsequent creatures. In this sense, emanation means that God uses instrumental causes in creating creatures out of nothing. 3) Emanation can mean that God creates, not by His own free choice, but necessarily, because it is a necessary consequence of His nature that He do so. This sort of causality is usually called *necessary emanation* and implies that the world is eternally caused by God.

essence, *quiddity*, or *nature*

These terms can all be used synonymously, and they can mean the same also as *form*. They are the terms used to express what a thing is; the answer given to the question, "what is it?" is an expression of the essence, quiddity, or nature of the thing. These terms, however, can differ from the term "form" in indicating not just the form alone but the form and matter together. The form alone is not what the thing is, for the thing is a composite of form and matter; to express the thing completely as a composite of form and matter, the term essence, quiddity, or nature is used. So the essence of man is thus to be both soul (form) and body (matter). The form of man alone would not be the essence of man. In this sense, "essence," "quiddity," or "nature" is often contrasted with *existence* or *being*. The essence of all creatures is really distinct from their existence or being. In God, however, essence and existence are one and the same.

eternity

In the strict sense, eternity means the sort of duration that is God's: a non-successive, totally actual existence. There is no prior or posterior, before or after, in God's eternal duration. In the looser sense, eternity means the unending duration of time. This may be considered in the past or in the future; hence one may speak about an eternal past (as a hypothetical possibility) or about an eternal future. In addition, some theologians will talk about a kind of eternity, sometimes called "eviternity," between God's eternity and eternal time, that is appropriate to the duration of angels.

faculty: see *power*

faith

An objective, definable doctrine, which tells us about God and man's relation to God, which in principle cannot be known by reason alone, and to which the intellect of man may assent. Such assent of the intellect is the result of God's grace.

final cause: see *cause*

form and *matter*

All physical things, or all things in the material world, are composed of two principles, form and matter. This is so because all things have two fundamental ways of being. On the one hand, things are actual and intelligible. What makes the thing actual and intelligible is its form. We know, for example, a bee by knowing its form. On the other hand, things are potentially other than they are, and they are unique individuals that resist our understanding, since understanding, properly speaking, concerns universals. What a bee is, for example, is not what *this* bee is. The potentiality and individuality of a thing is caused by its matter. That a thing is real or actual, and that a thing can be understood, classified, and analyzed – this is all caused by its form. That a thing is potentially changed, that it is different from all others, that it is incomprehensible – all this is from its matter. All physical things have both sorts of characteristics, both those that derive from the form and those that derive from the matter, and hence all physical things must be composites of form and matter. Form and matter are not *things* but are, rather, correlative *principles* of things. In the physical world there is no such thing as form without matter or matter without form. Matter in its most basic sense is called *prime matter*, the basic underlying substrate of all substantial change. Usually, however, we refer to matter in a secondary sense, according to which we mean the identifiable elements or materials out of which something is composed.

formal cause: see *cause*

genus and *species*

These are terms to indicate categories relative to one another. Thus, a genus is the broader category and the species is the narrower category or the sub-category. A chemical element, for example, is a genus, and hydrogen, gold, or sulphur are examples of species within the genus. Or, we could divide things differently and say that metal is the genus and that gold, silver, aluminum, etc. are species. A genus and a species express essences, quiddities, natures, or forms; the genus is the more general essence, and the species is the more specific essence.

immaterial: see *material*

incorruptible: see *corruptible*

infinite

That which has no limits, or that of which there may always be more. Aristotle argues that no physical thing can be actually infinite. Potentially, a physical thing may be considered infinite only in the sense that matter is infinitely divisible (in principle, though not in practice) or in the sense that time might be infinite. In actuality, only God is infinite.

infinite regress

A defect in arguing or in explaining such that the argument or explanation given has no logical conclusion. If someone says that A is caused by B, and that B is caused by C, and that C is caused by D, and so forth, such that there is no end to the causes, then an infinite regress is being proposed. Such, however, is really no explanation at all.

intelligence: see *angel*

local motion: see *change*

material and *immaterial*

That which is material is made out of matter; that which is immaterial is not made out of any matter. Thus a material substance is a composite of form and matter. An immaterial substance, as it has no matter, is simply a form.

material cause: see *cause*

matter: see *form*

metaphysics

The most general philosophical science of all of reality. Whatever is real is being; hence metaphysics is the science of being. Since what is real includes material and immaterial beings, metaphysics teaches what is true about being, in a general way, for both material and immaterial things. Aristotle and Aquinas understood meta-physics to be a science, that is, to give real demonstrations.

motion: see *change*

natural philosophy: see *physics*

nature: see *essence*

necessary or *necessity*

In general, that which is necessary cannot be otherwise. There are a number of senses of this term that are philosophically important, but two are particularly relevant here. Something may be neces-sary in itself or necessary through another. Absolutely, only God is necessary through Himself, for only God exists necessarily (or cannot not exist). All creatures exist through God's causality, and, given that causality, they must necessarily exist. In that sense, creatures are all necessary through another. However, considered in themselves, without reference to God's causality, it is possible to say that some creatures are necessary through themselves, for there is nothing about them that would make them liable to disso-lution. Thus, immaterial substances are necessary in themselves, for they are not liable to dissolution.

necessary emanation: see *emanation*

order of duration, order of nature; (or *priority in nature, priority in duration*)

Things can be ordered in duration, that is, ordered in time. If so, something may be prior to something else because it is earlier. On the other hand, things can be ordered in nature, in the sense that one thing is more important or more basic or more fundamental than something else. In other words, the terms "before and after," or "prior and posterior" can apply either to duration (temporal) or to nature (importance in being).

passive potency: see *active potency*

physics or *natural philosophy*

The general science of material beings which, because they are material, are capable of motion. Hence, physics is the science of movable being. Aristotle and Aquinas understand physics to be a general science of nature, concerned with nature, time, motion, and the like (and not an experimental science that requires special-ized techniques and equipment), and yet to be a science, for it of-fers demonstrations. Today, the term physics is used more nar-rowly to mean a mathematical and experimental science.

potency, potential, potentiality: see *act*
power or *faculty*
> The ability that something has for doing something. Synonym: *active potency.*

prime matter
> The basic underlying substrate of all substantial change. Prime matter is not knowable or identifiable in itself. It is matter in its most basic sense. See also *matter.*

principle
> A principle is that from which something else comes in some way or another; it is a "first" in some sense. The term principle is a genus in which the term cause is a species. All causes are principles, but not all principles are causes. God is the first principle of the world, which means that He is the first cause of the whole world, but it also means that He is the first being. Some principles are not causes: a point, for example, is the principle of a line, in the sense that it is a more basic reality needed for the reality of a line, but a line is not caused by a point (or even by a set of points). A line is not made up of points. See also *cause.*

priority in duration: see *order of duration*
priority in nature: see *order of nature*
privative: see *contraries*
probable argument: see *demonstration*
quiddity: see *essence*
science
> Any organized body of knowledge that gives demonstrative knowledge through causes is a science. Metaphysics and natural philosophy, contemporary mathematical physics, biology, and theology are sciences. To be a science, a doctrine must give fundamental explanations of why things are as they are.

separate intelligence: see *angel*
separated substance: see *angel*
sophistical argument: see *demonstration*
species: see *genus*
subject: see *substance*
substance and *accident*
> A substance is that which exists independently; it does not exist in something as in a subject, or it does not inhere in something else.

Thus a human being, a tree, a rock, or a drop of water are all examples of substances. An accident, on the other hand, can only exist in or inhere in some subject or substance. Thus, a color, a shape, a quantity, a relation, when something is, where it is, etc. are realities that inhere in independently existing substances. An accident is that which exists in something else as in a subject. The term *subject* may often be used as a synonym for substance, but it can be used in a more restricted sense to mean a part of a substance. Thus, a person's ideas are in his intellect, as in a subject, but his intellect is not a substance. Note that according to Thomas Aquinas, a substance is a substance because it possesses a *substantial form*, and an accident is an accident because of an *accidental form*. Substances, therefore, are composites of matter (prime matter) and substantial form, and accidents are accidental forms that inhere in substances.

Bibliography

ABBREVIATIONS

CCL   Corpus Christianorum. Series Latina. Turnhout: Brepols, 1953– .
CSEL   Corpus scriptorum ecclesiasticorum latinorum. Vienna: F. Temp-
        sky, and various imprints, 1866– .
PG   Patrologiae cursus completus. Series Graeca. Ed. J.-P. Migne. 161
        vols. Paris: Migne, 1857–1866. Various reprints.
PL   Patrologiae cursus completus. Series Latina. Ed. J.-P. Migne. 221
        vols. Paris: Migne, 1844–1864. Various reprints.

PRIMARY SOURCES

Albert. *Opera omnia.* Ed. Auguste Borgnet. 38 vols. Paris: Ludovico Vivès,
    1890–1899.
al-Ghazālī [Algazel]. *Tahāfut al-Falāsifah.* 1 Texte Arabe établi et accom-
    pagné d'un sommaire Latin et d'un index par Maurice Bouyges. Bib-
    liotheca Arabica Scholasticorum, série Arabe, 2. Beirut: Imprimerie
    Catholique, 1927. 2 Trans. Sabih Ahmad Kamali as *Tahāfut al-Falā-
    sifah (Incoherence of the Philosophers).* Lahore: Pakistan Philosophical
    Congress, [1958].
Anselm. *Opera Omnia.* 1 Ed. Francis S. Schmitt, 6 vols. Edinburgh: Thom-
    as Nelson, 1938–1961. 2 Trans. Jasper Hopkins and Herbert W. Rich-
    ardson as *Anselm of Canterbury.* 4 vols. Toronto and New York: Ed-
    win Mellen Press, 1974–1976.
Augustine. *De doctrina christiana* 1 PL 34: 15–122. 2 Ed. Joseph Martin.
    CCL 32 [1982]: 1–167. 3 Trans. D.W. Robertson as *On Christian Doc-
    trine.* Indianapolis, IN: Bobbs-Merrill, 1958.
–. *Confessiones.* 1 PL 32: 659–868. 2 Ed. Lucas Verheijen. CCL 27 [1981].
    Trans. R.S. Pine-Coffin as *Confessions.* Harmondsworth, UK: Penguin,
    1961.
–. *De Civitate Dei.* 1 PL 41: 13–804. 2 Ed. Bernard Dombart and Alphonse
    Kalb. CCL 47–48 [1955]. 3 Trans. Henry Bettenson as *Concerning the
    City of God Against the Pagans.* Harmondsworth, UK: Penguin, 1972

–. *Contra Faustum Manichaeum.* **1** Ed. Josph Zycha. CSEL 25.1: 248–797. Trans. Richard Stothert as "Reply to Faustus the Manichean." In *Nicene and Post-Nicene Fathers* [first series], ed. Philip Schaff, 4: 151–365. New York: Christian Literature Company, 1886–1890.

–. *De Genesi ad litteram.* **1** PL 34: 245–486. **2** Ed. Joseph Zycha, CSEL 28.1 [1894]: 1–456. **3** Trans. John Taylor as *The Literal Meaning of Genesis.* Ancient Christian Writers 41–42. 2 vols. New York: Newman Press, 1982.

–. *De Trinitate.* **1** PL 42: 819–1098. **2** Ed. W.J. Mountain and Fr. Glorie. 2 vols. CCL 50a–b [1968]. **3** Trans. Stephen McKenna as *The Trinity.* The Fathers of the Church 45. Washington, DC: The Catholic University of America Press, 1963.

Averroes. *Aristotelis opera cum Averrois commentariis.* Venice: Apud Junctas, 1562–1574.

–. *Commentarium magnum in Aristotelis libros De anima.* Ed. F. Stuart Crawford. Cambridge, MA: The Mediaeval Academy of America, 1953.

–. *Tahāfut al-Tahāfut.* **1** Texte Arabe établi par Maurice Bourges. Bibliotheca Arabica Scholasticorum, série Arabe, 3. Beirut: Imprimerie Catholique, 1930. **2** Trans. Simon Van den Bergh as *Averroes' Tahafut al-Tahafut (The Incoherence of the Incoherence).* 2 vols. London: Messers. Luzac and Company, 1954.

–. *Averroes' De substantia orbis.* Critical edition of the Hebrew text with English translation and commentary by Arthur Hyman. Medieval Academy Books 96; Corpus philosophorum Medii Aevi. Cambridge, MA: Medieval Academy of America; Jerusalem: Israel Academy of Sciences and the Humanities, 1986.

Avicenna. *De causis primis et secundis et de fluxu qui consequitur eas.* In Roland de Vaux, *Notes et texts sur l'Avicennisme latin aux confins des XIIe et XIIIe siècles,* pp. 97–102. Bibliotheque thomiste 20, section historique 17. Paris: J. Vrin, 1934.

–. *Opera philosophica.* Venice: [s.n.], 1508. Repr., Louvain: Édition de la bibliothèque SJ, 1961.

–. *Ibn Sīnā: al-Shifā' al-Ilāhiyyāt (La Métaphysique).* **1** Édition critique du texte arabe, ed. Georges Anawati et al. 2 vols. Cairo: Imprimerie Nationale, Ministère de l'Education Nationale, 1960. **2** Trans. Georges C. Anawati in Avicenne, *La Métaphysique du Shifā',* Études Musulmanes 21, 27. 2 vols. Paris: J. Vrin, 1978–1985.

–. *Liber de philosophia prima sive scientia divina.* 3 vols. Ed. S. Van Riet. Louvain: E. Peeters; Leiden: E.J. Brill, 1977–1983.

–. *Avicenna's psychology: An English translation of Kitab al-Najat, Book II, Chapter VI.* Ed. Fazlur Rahman. London: Oxford University Press, 1952.

Boethius. *Philosophiae Consolatio.* PL 63: 579–802. **2** Ed. William Weinberger, CSEL 57 [1934]. **2** Ed. Ludovico Bieler. CCL 94 [1957]. **3** Trans. S.J. Tester as "The Consolation of Philosophy," in *Boethius*, 2nd ed. Loeb Classical Library. Cambridge, MA: Harvard University Press; London: Heinemann, 1973.

Boethius of Daccia. *On the Supreme Good; On the Eternity of the World; On Dreams.* Mediaeval Sources in Translation 30. Trans. John Wippel. Toronto: Pontifical Institute of Mediaeval Studies, 1987.

Bonaventure. *Opera omnia.* Ed. The Fathers of the College of St. Bonaventure. 10 vols. Quracchi: Collegium S. Bonaventurae, 1882–1902.

Dionysius the Areopagite. *De coelesti hierarchia.* **1** PG 3: 119–370. **2** Ed. Günter Heil, trans. Maurice de Gandillac as *La hiérarchie céleste.* Sources chrétiennes 58. 1958. 2nd ed. Paris: Editions du Cerf, 1970. **3** Ed. Günter Heil. In Corpus Dionysiacum 2: Patristische Texte und Studien 36. Berlin and New York: Walter de Gruyter, 1991. **4** Trans. the editors of the Shrine of Wisdom. *The Mystical Theology and the Celestial Hierarchies of Dionysius the Areopagite.* North Godalming, Surrey: The Shrine of Wisdom, 1949.

–. *De divinis nominibus.* **1** PG 3: 586–996. **2** Ed. Beate Regina Suchla. In Corpus Dionysiacum 1: Patristische Texte und Studien 33. Berlin and New York: Walter de Gruyter, 1990. **2** Trans. John D. Jones as *The Divine Names and Mystical Theology.* Milwaukee, WI: Marquette University Press, 1980.

Enchiridion Symbolorum. Ed. Heinric Denzinger. Editio 18–20. Freiburg: Herder, 1932.

Hippolytus. *Refutatio omnium haeresium.* **1** In PG 16: 3009–5468. **2** Ed. Miroslav Marcovich. Patristische Texte und Studien 25. Berlin and New York: Walter de Gruyter, 1986. **3** Trans. As "The Refutation of All Heresies," in *The Ante-Nicene Fathers*, ed. Alexander Roberts and James Donaldson, 9 vols., 5: 9–153. Buffalo: Christian Literature Company, 1885–1903.

Hugh of St. Victor. *De sacramentis Christianae fidei libri duo.* **1** PL 176: 173–618. **2** Trans. Roy J. Deferrari as *Hugh of St. Victor on the Sacraments of* *the Christian Faith.* Cambridge, MA: Medieval Academy of America, 1951.

John Damascene. *De fide orthodoxa.* 1 Ed. Eligius M. Buytaert. Franciscan Institute Publications 8. St. Bonaventure, NY: The Franciscan Institute, 1955. 2 Trans. Frederic H. Chase as "The Orthodox Faith," in John of Damascus, *Writings.* Fathers of the Church 37. New York: Fathers of the Church, 1958.

John Philoponus. *Against Aristotle on the Eternity of the World.* Trans. Christian Wildberg. Ithaca, NY: Cornell University Press, 1987.

Liber de causis. 1 Ed. Adriaan Pattin. Louvain: Tijdschrift voor Filosophie, 1966. 2 Trans. Dennis J. Brand as *The Book of Causes.* Niagara, NY: Niagara University Press, 1981.

Maimonides. *Dalalat al-ḥa'irīn (Guide of the Perplexed).* 1 Arabic text based on the text of Salomon Munk; ed. Issagar Joel. Jerusalem: Junovitch, 1929. 2 Trans. Shlomo Pines as *The Guide of the Perplexed.* Chicago: University of Chicago Press, 1963.

[Paris, University of.] *Chartularium Universitatis Parisiensis.* Ed. Heinrich Denifle and Emile Chatelain. 4 vols. Paris: Delalain, 1889–1897.

Peter Lombard. *Sententiae in IV Libris distinctae.* Ed. Ignatius Brady. 2 vols. Rome: Collegium S. Bonaventurae, 1971–1981.

Simplicius. *Against Philoponus on the Eternity of the World.* Trans. Christian Wildberg. In *Place, Void, and Eternity,* ed. C. Wildberg and David J. Furley, pp. 97–141. Ithaca, NY: Cornell University Press, 1991.

Thomas Aquinas. *Opera omnia, iussu impensaque Leonis XIII P.M. edita* [the Leonine edition]. Rome: Commissio Leonina, and various imprints, 1882– .

–. *Compendium theologiae.* 1 Ed. Raimondo Verardo. In *Opuscula theologica,* 1: 9–138. 2 vols. Turin: Marietti, 1954. 2 Trans. Cyril Vollert as *Compendium of Theology.* London; St. Louis: B. Herder Book Co., 1947.

–. *Expositio in duodecim libros Metaphysicorum Aristotelis.* 1 Ed. M.-R. Cathala and Raimondo Spiazzi. Turin: Marietti, 1950. 2 Trans. John P. Rowan as *Commentary on the Metaphysics of Aristotle.* 2 vols. Chicago: H. Regnery, 1961. Repr. Notre Dame, IN: Dumb Ox Books, 1995.

–. *De aeternitate mundi.* 1 In the Leonine edition of the *Opera omnia,* vol. 43 [1976], pp. 49–89. 2 Trans. Cyril Vollert. In Aquinas, *On the Eternity of the World.* [with works by Siger of Brabant and St. Bonaventure]. Mediaeval Philosophical Texts in Translation 16. Milwaukee: Marquette University Press, 1964. **3** Trans. Baldner–Carroll in Appendix B, pp. 114–122 above.

–. *De articulis fidei et ecclesiae sacramentis.* In the Leonine edition of the *Opera omnia,* vol. 42 [1979], pp. 207–257.

–. *De substantiis separatiis.* **1** Ed. H.-F. Dondaine. In the Leonine edition of the *Opera omnia,* vol. 40 [1969], pp. 1D–87D. **2** Trans. Francis J. Lescoe as *Treatise on Separate Substances.* West Hartford, CT: St. Joseph College, 1959.

–. *Expositio in Aristoelis libros De caelo et mundo.* **1** Ed. Raymondo M. Spiazzi. Turin: Marietti, 1952. **2** Trans. R.F. Larcher and Pierre Conway as *Exposition of Aristotle's Treatise on the Heavens.* Columbus, OH: College of St. Mary of the Springs, 1963.

–. *Expositio in octos libros Physicorum Aristotelis.* **1** Ed. P.M. Maggiolo. Turin: Marietti, 1965. **2** Trans. Richard J. Blackwell, et al. New Haven, CT: Yale University Press, 1963.

–. *Expositio super primam et secundum decretalem.* Ed. H.-F. Dondaine. In the Leonine edition of the *Opera omnia,* vol. 40 [1969], pp. E1–E50.

–. *Quaestiones de quolibet.* Ed. H.-F. Dondaine, in the Leonine edition of the *Opera omnia,* vol. 25 [1996]. **2** Trans. Sandra Edwards as *Quodlibetal Questions 1 and 2.* Mediaeval Sources in Translation 27. Toronto: Pontifical Institute of Mediaeval Studies, 1983.

–. *Quaestiones disputatae De potentia Dei.* **1** Ed. P.M. Pession. In *Quaestiones disputatae,* ed. Raimondo Spiazzi, 1: 1–276. 9th ed. 2 vols. Turin: Marietti, 1953. **2** Trans. Lawrence Shapcote as *On the Power of God.* 3 vols. London: Burns, Oates, and Washbourne, 1932–1934.

–. *Scriptum super libros Sententiarum Petri Lombardi.* Eds. P. Mandonnet and M.F. Moos. 4 vols. Paris: P. Lethielleux, 1929–1947.

–. *Summa contra Gentiles.* **1** Ed. Ceslas Pera, Pietro Marc, and Pietro Caramello. 3 vols. Turin: Marietti, 1961–1967. **2** Trans. A.C. Pegis et al. as *On the Truth of the Catholic Faith.* Garden City, NY: Image Books, 1955–1957. Repr. as *Summa contra Gentiles.* 4 vols. Notre Dame, IN: University of Notre Dame Press, 1975.

–. *Summa theologiae.* **1** Ed. Institutum Studiorum Medievalium Ottaviensis. 5 vols. Ottawa: Studium Generalis O. Pr., 1941–1945. **2** Trans. Timothy McDermott as *Summa theologiae: A Concise Translation.* Westminister, MD: Christian Classics, 1989.

–. *Super Librum de causis expositio.* **1** Ed. Henri-Dominique Saffrey. Fribourg: Société Philosophique, 1954. **2** Trans. and annotated by Vincent A. Gualiardo, Charles R. Hess, and Richard C. Taylor as *Commentary on the Book of Causes*. Washington, DC: The Catholic University of America Press, 1996.

SECONDARY SOURCES

Abed, Shukri B. *Aristotelian Logic and the Arabic Language in Al-Fārābī*. Albany: State University of New York Press, 1991.

Aertsen, Jan. *Nature and Creature: Thomas Aquinas's Way of Thought.* [Trans. from the Dutch by Herbert Donald Morton.] Studien und Texte zur Geistesgeschichte des Mittelalters 21. Leiden: E.J. Brill, 1988.

Aillet, Marc. *Lire la Bible avec S. Thomas*. Fribourg: Éditions Universitaires, 1993.

Alter, Robert; and Frank Kermode, ed. *The Literary Guide to the Bible.* Cambridge, MA: Harvard University Press, 1987.

Anawati, Georges. "St. Thomas d'Aquin et la Métaphysique d'Avicenne. In *St. Thomas Aquinas, 1274–1974, Commemorative Studies*, ed. Armand Maurer et al., 1: 449–465. Toronto: Pontifical Institute of Mediaeval Studies, 1974.

–. *Islam et christianisme: La rencontre de deux cultures en Occidente au Moyen-Âge*. Cairo: Institut Dominicain d'Etudes Orientales, 1991.

Anderson, James F. *The Cause of Being. The Philosophy of Creation in St. Thomas Aquinas*. London: Herder, 1952.

Argerami, Omar. "La question *De aeternitate mundi*: Posiciones Doctrinales." *Sapientia* 27 (Oct.-Dec. 1972): 313–334.

–. "Metafísica y experencia en la escolástica del siglo xiii." *Revista Latinoamerica de Filosofia* 5 (nd): 43–52.

Arnaldez, Roger. "L'histoire de la pensée grecque vue par les Arabes." *Bulletin de la societe francaise de philosophie* 72 (1978): 117–168.

–. *À la croisée des trois monothéismes: Une communauté de pensée au Moyen Âge*. Paris: Albin Michel, 1993.

"Avicenna." In *Encyclopaedia Iranica*, 3: 66–110. London and New York: Routledge & Kegan Paul, 1989.

Baldner, Steven. "St. Bonaventure on the Temporal Beginning of the World." *The New Scholasticism* 63 (1989): 206–228.

Basti, Gianfranco; and Antonio Perrone. *Le radici forti del pensiero debole dalla metafisica, alla matematica, al calcolo*. Percorsi della scienza 7. Padova: Il poligrafo; Rome: Pontificia Università Lateranense, 1996.

Beierwaltes, Walter. *Platonismus in der Philosophie des Mittelalters.* Wege der Forschung 197. Darmstadt: Wissenchaftliche Buchgesellschaft, 1969.

Bertola, Ermenegildo. "Tommaso D'Aquino e il problema dell'eternità del mondo." *Rivista di Filosofia Neo-Scolastica* 66 (1974): 312–355.

Bianchi, Luca. "Bibliografia sul problema dell'eternità del mondo nella scolastica (secoli XII-XIV)." *Bollettino* 3–4 (1984): 130–134.

–. *L'errore di Aristotele: La polemica contro l'eternità del mondo nel XIII secolo.* Firenze: La Nuova Italia Editrice, 1984.

–. *L'inizio dei tempi: antichità e novità del mondo da Bonaventura a Newton.* Firenze: Leo Olschki, 1987.

–. *Le verità dissonanti: Aristotele alla fine del Medioevo.* Roma: Laterza, 1990.

–. *Il Vescovo e i Filosofi: La condanna parigiana del 1277 e l'evoluzione dell'aristotelismo scolastico.* Bergamo: Pierluigi Lubrina Editrice, 1990.

Black, Deborah L. "Averroës." In *Dictionary of Literary Biography,* vol. 115 (*Medieval Philosophers,* ed. Jeremiah Hackett), pp. 68–79. Detroit: Gale Research, 1992.

Bonansea, Bernardo. "The Question of an Eternal World in the Teaching of St. Bonaventure." *Franciscan Studies* 34 (1974): 7–33.

Booth, Edward. *Aristotelian Aporetic Ontology in Islamic and Christian Thinkers.* Cambridge Studies in Medieval Life and Thought, 3rd series, 20. Cambridge: Cambridge University Press, 1984.

Bosley, Richard; and Martin Tweedale, ed. *Aristotle and His Medieval Interpreters.* Alberta: University of Calgary Press, 1992.

Brady, Ignatius. "Pierre Lombard." In *Dictionnaire de spiritualité,* ed. Marcel Viller et al., 12: 1604–1612. 16 vols. and index. Paris: Beauchesne, 1932–1995.

Brown, Stephen F. "The Eternity of the World Discussion in Early Oxford." In *Mensch und Natur im Mittelalter,* ed. A. Zimmermann and A. Speer, 1: 259–280.

Buckley, Michael. *Motion and Motion's God .* Princeton, NJ: Princeton University Press, 1981.

Burrell, David B. *Knowing the Unknowable God: Ibn Sīnā, Maimonides, Aquinas.* Notre Dame, IN: University of Notre Dame Press, 1986.

–. "Aquinas and Islamic and Jewish Thinkers." In *The Cambridge Companion to Aquinas,* ed. N. Kretzmann and E. Stump, pp. 60–84.

–. *Freedom and Creation in Three Traditions.* Notre Dame, IN: University of Notre Dame Press, 1994.

–; and Bernard McGinn, ed. *God and Creation.* Notre Dame, IN: University of Notre Dame Press, 1990.

Butterworth, Charles; and Blake André Kessel, ed. *The Introduction of Arabic Philosophy into Europe.* Studien und Texte zur Geistesgeschichte des Mittelalters 39. Leiden: E.J. Brill, 1994.

Carroll, William E. "Big Bang Cosmology, Quantum Tunneling from Nothing, and Creation." *Laval théologique et philosophique* 44 (1988): 59–75.

–. "S. Tommaso, Aristotele, e la creazione." *Annales Theologici* 8 (1994): 365–376.

Chenu, M.-D. "La condition de créature: Sur trois textes de saint Thomas." *Archives d'histoire doctrinale et littéraire du moyen âge* 37 (1970): 9–16.

–. *Nature, Man, and Society in the Twelfth Century.* Trans. Jerome Taylor and Lester K. Little. Chicago: The University of Chicago Press, 1968.

Colish, Marcia. *Peter Lombard.* 2 vols. Leiden: E.J. Brill, 1994.

Cottier, Georges. "Le concept de nature chez Saint Thomas." In *Physica, Cosmologia, Naturphilosophie: Nuovi Approcci,* ed. Marcello Sorondo, pp. 37–64. Roma: Herder — Università Lateranense, 1993.

Dales, Richard C. *Medieval Discussions of the Eternity of the World.* Leiden: E. J. Brill, 1990.

–; and Omar Argerami, ed. *Medieval Latin Texts on the Eternity of the World.* Leiden: E.J. Brill, 1991.

Davidson, Herbert. *Proofs for Eternity, Creation, and the Existence of God in Medieval Islamic and Jewish Philosophy.* Oxford: Oxford University Press, 1987.

–. *Al-Fārābī, Avicenna, and Averroes, on Intellect: Their Cosmologies, Theories of the Active Intellect, and Theories of the Human Intellect.* Oxford: Oxford University Press, 1992.

Davies, Brian. *The Thought of Thomas Aquinas.* Oxford: The Clarendon Press, 1992.

de Corte, Marcel. "La Causalité du Premier Moteur dans la Philosophie Aristotélicienne." *Revue d'Histoire de la Philosophie* 5 (1931): 8–146.

Dewan, Lawrence. "St. Albert, Creation, and the Philosophers." *Laval théologique et philosophique* 40 (1984): 295–307.

–. "St. Thomas, Aristotle, and Creation." *Dionysius* 15 (1991): 81–90.

–. "Thomas Aquinas, Creation, and Two Historians." *Laval théologique et philosophique* 50 (1994): 363–387.

Dhanani, Almoor. *The Physical Theory of Kalam: Atoms, Space, and Void in Basrian Mu'tazli Cosmology.* Leiden: E.J. Brill, 1994.

Dodds, Michael J. *The Unchanging God of Love: A Study of the Teaching of St. Thomas Aquinas on Divine Immutability in View of Certain Contemporary Criticism of This Doctrine.* Fribourg: Éditions Universitaires, 1986.

Druart, Thérèse-Anne. "The Soul and Body Problem: Avicenna and Descartes." In *Arabic Philosophy and the West,* ed. T.-A. Druart, pp. 27–49. Washington, DC: Georgetown University Press, 1988.

–. "Al-Fārābī and Emanationism." In *Studies in Medieval Philosophy,* ed. John Wippel, pp. 23–43. Studies in Philosophy and the History of Philosophy 17. Washington, DC: The Catholic University of America Press, 1987.

Dümplemann, Leo. *Kreation als ontisch-ontologisches Verhältnis. Zur Metaphysik des Schopfungstheologie des Thomas von Aquin.* Freiburg: K. Alber, 1969.

Elders, Leo J. *La Filosofia della Natura di San Tommaso d'Aquino.* Roma: Libreria Editrice Vaticana, 1996.

Emery, G. "Le Père et l'oeuvre trinitaire de création selon le Commentaire des Sentences de S. Thomas d'Aquin." In *Ordo sapientiae et amoris: Image et message de saint Thomas d'Aquin à travers les récentes études historiques, herméneutiques et doctrinales,* ed. Carlos Josaphat Pinto de Oliveira, pp. 85–117. Fribourg, Switzerland: Editions Universitaires Fribourg, 1993.

Emery, Kent. "*Sapientissimus Aristotelis* and *Theologicissimus Dionysius*: The Reading of Aristotle and the Understanding of Nature in Denys the Carthusian." In *Mensch und Natur im Mittelalter,* ed. A. Zimmermann and A. Speer, 2: 572–606.

Fabro, Corenlio. "Platonism, Neo-Platonism, and Thomism: Convergences and Divergences." *The New Scholasticism* 44 (1970): 69–100.

Fackenheim, Emil. "The Possibility of the Universe in Al-Fārābī, Ibn Sīnā, and Maimonides." *Proceedings of the American Academy for Jewish Research* 16 (1947): 39–70.

Feldman, Seymour. "The Theory of Eternal Creation in Hasdai Crescas and Some of His Predecessors," *Viator* 11 (1980):. 289–320.

Fitzmyer, Joseph A. *The Biblical Commission's Document 'The Interpretation of the Bible in the Church': Text and Commentary.* Subsidia Biblica 18. Rome: Editrice Pontificio Biblico, 1995.

Flasch, Kurt. *Aufklärung im Mittelalter? Die Verurteilung von 1277. Das Dokument des Bischofs von Paris*. Mainz: Dieterich, 1989.

Forni, Guglielmo. *La filosofia Cristiana: una discussione (1927–33) appunti del corso 1987–88*. Bologna: CLUEB, 1988.

Fox, Marvin. *Interpreting Maimonides: Studies in Methodology, Metaphysics, and Moral Philosophy*. Chicago: The University of Chicago Press, 1990.

Frank, Richard. "The Origin of the Arabic Philosophical Term *anniua*." *Cahiers de Byrsa*. 6 (1956): 181–201.

–. *Creation and the Cosmic System: Al-Ghazālī and Avicenna*. Heidelberg: Carl Winter, 1992.

–. *Al-Ghazālī and the Ash'arite School*. Durham, North Carolina: Duke University Press, 1994.

Freddoso, Alfred. "God's General Concurrence with Secondary Causes: Pitfalls and Prospects." *American Catholic Philosophical Quarterly* 68 (1994): 131–156.

Gerson, Lloyd. *Plotinus*. London and New York: Routledge, 1994.

Ghisalberti, Alessandro. *Medioevo Teologico*. Roma: Laterza, 1990.

Gilson, Etienne. *Being and Some Philosophers*. 2nd ed. Toronto: Pontifical Institute of Mediaeval Studies, 1952.

–. *A History of Christian Philosophy in the Middle Ages*. London: Sheed and Ward, 1955.

–. *The Christian Philosophy of St. Augustine*. Trans. L.E.M. Lynch. London: Victor Gollancz, 1961.

–. *The Christian Philosophy of St. Thomas Aquinas*. Trans. L.K. Shook. New York: Random House, 1956.

–. *Christian Philosophy*. Trans. Armand Maurer. Etienne Gilson Series 17. Toronto: Pontifical Institute of Mediaeval Studies, 1993.

Gisel, Pierre. *La création*. Paris: Labor et Fides, 1987.

Goichon, Amélie-Marie. *La distinction de l'essence et de l'existence d'après Ibn Sīnā (Avicenne)*. Paris: Desclée de Brouwer, 1937.

Goodman, Lenn E. *Avicenna*. London: Routledge, 1992.

–, ed. *Neoplatonism and Jewish Thought*. Studies in Neoplatonism 7. Albany: State University of New York Press, 1992.

Grabmann, Martin. *Der lateinische Averroismus des 13. Jahrhunderts und seine Stellung zur christlichen Weltanschauung*. Munich: Bayerische Akademie der Wissenchaften, 1931.

Grant, Edward. *Planets, Stars, and Orbs. The Medieval Cosmos, 1200–1687*. Cambridge: Cambridge University Press, 1994.

–. *The Foundations of Modern Science in the Middle Ages: Their Religious, Institutional, and Intellectual Contexts.* Cambridge: Cambridge University Press, 1996.

Guitton, Jean . *Le temps et l'éternité chez Plotin et saint Augustin.* 4th ed. Paris: J. Vrin: 1971·

Gutas, Dimitri. *Avicenna and the Aristotelian Tradition.* Leiden: E.J. Brill, 1988.

Hankey, W.J. "Theology as System and as Science: Proclus and Thomas Aquinas." *Dionysius* 6 (1982): 83–93.

Henley, R.J. *Saint Thomas and Platonism: A Study of the 'Plato' and the 'Platonic' Texts in the Writings of Saint Thomas.* The Hague: Martinus Nijhoff, 1956.

Henninger, Mark G. "Aquinas on the Ontological Status of Relations." *Journal of the History of Philosophy* 25 (1987): 491–515.

Hissette, Roland. *Enquête sur les 219 articles condamnés à Paris le 7 mars 1277.* Louvain: Publications Universitaires, 1977.

–. "Étienne Tempier et ses condamnations." *Recherches de théologie ancienne et médiévale* 47 (1980): 231–270.

–. "Albert le Grand et Thomas d'Aquin dans la censure parisienne du 7 mars 1277." In *Studien zur Mittelalterlichen Geistesgeschichte und Ihren Quellen,* ed. Albert Zimmermann, pp. 226–246. Berlin: Walter de Gruyter, 1982.

Hossfeld, Paul. "Gott und die Welt. Zum achten Buch der Physik des Albertus Magnus (nach dem kritisch erstellen Text)." In *Mensch und Natur im Mittelalter,* ed. A. Zimmermann and A. Speer, 1: 281–301.

Hourani, George F. "Ibn Sīnā on Necessary and Possible Existence." *Philosophical Forum* 4 (1972–1973): 74–86.

Hyman, Arthur; and James Walsh. *Philosophy in the Middle Ages: The Christian, Islamic, and Jewish Traditions.* 2nd ed. Indianapolis: Hackett, 1987.

Ivry, Alfred. "Maimonides on Creation." In *Creation and the End of Days: Judaism and Scientific Cosmology,* ed. David Novak and Robert Samuelson, pp. 185–213. Lanham, MD: University Press of America, 1986.

Jaki, Stanley. *Genesis 1 Through the Ages.* London: Thomas More Press, 1992.

Johnson, Mark. "Did St. Thomas Attribute a Doctrine of Creation to Aristotle?" *The New Scholasticism* 63 (1989): 129–155.

Jolivet, Jean. "Aristote et la notion de création." *Revue des sciences philosophiques et théologiques* 19 (1930): 209–235.

–, ed. *Multiple Averroès: Actes du Colloque International organisé à l'occasion du 850ᵉ anniversaire de la naissance d'Avveroès, Paris 20–23 novembre 1976.* Paris: Belles Lettres, 1978.

Kahn, Charles H. "Why Existence Does Not Emerge as a Distinct Concept in Greek Philosophy." In *Philosophies of Existence: Ancient and Medieval*, ed. by Parviz Morewedge, pp. 7–17. Bronx, NY: Fordham University Press, 1982.

Kellner, Menachem. "On the Status of the Astronomy and Physics in Maimonides' *Mishneh Torah* and *Guide of the Perplexed*: A Chapter in the History of Science." *British Journal of the History of Science* 24 (1991): 453–463.

–. *Maimonides on Human Perfection.* Atlanta: Scholars Press, 1990.

Knasas, John F.X. "Aquinas' Ascription of Creation to Aristotle." *Angelicum* 73 (1996): 487–506.

Kogan, Barry S. *Averroes and the Metaphysics of Causation.* Binghamton, NY: State University of New York Press, 1985.

Kovach, Francis. "The Question of the Eternity of the World in St. Bonaventure and St. Thomas: A Critical Analysis." *Southwestern Journal of Philosophy* 5 (1974): 141–172.

Kretzmann, Norman. *The Metaphysics of Theism.* Oxford: Oxford University Press, 1997.

–; and Eleanor Stump, ed. *The Cambridge Companion to Aquinas.* Cambridge: Cambidge University Press, 1993.

Leaman, Oliver. *An Introduction to Medieval Islamic Philosophy.* Cambridge: Cambridge University Press, 1985.

–. *Moses Maimonides.* London: Routledge, 1990.

–. *Averroes and His Philosophy.* Oxford: Clarendon Press, 1988.

Leslie, John. *Universes.* New York: Routledge, 1989.

Long, R. James, ed. *Philosophy and the God of Abraham: Essays in Memory of James A. Weisheipl, OP.* Papers in Mediaeval Studies 12. Toronto: Pontifical Institute of Mediaeval Studies, 1991.

MacIntosh, J.J. "St. Thomas and the Traversal of the Infinite." *American Catholic Philosophical Quarterly* 68 (1994): 157–177.

Macken, R. "La temporalité radicale de la créature selon Henri de Gand." *Recherches de Théologie Ancienne et Mediévale* 38 (1971): 210–272.

Marengo, G. *Trinità e Creazione. Indagine sulla teologia di Tommaso d'Aquino.* Roma, 1990.

Marmura, Michael. "Avicenna's 'Flying Man' in Context." *The Monist* 69 (1986): 185–216.

–, ed. *Islamic Theology and Philosophy: Studies in Honor of Geroge F. Hourani.* Albany: State University of New York Press, 1984.

–. "Ghazālī's Chapter on Divine Power in the *Iqtisīd.*" *Arabic Sciences and Philosophy* 4 (1994): 279–315.

Margolióuth, Moses. "The Discussion between Abu Bishr Matta and Abu Sa'id al-Sirafi on the Merits of Logic and Grammar." *Journal of the Royal Asiatic Society,* ns 37 (1905): 79–129.

Martínez, Rafael, ed. *La verità scientifica.* Roma: Armanda Editore, 1995.

–. *Immagini del dinamismo fisico. Causa e tempo nella storia della scienza.* Roma: Armando Editore, 1996.

May, Gerhard. *'Creatio ex nihilo': The Doctrine of 'Creation out of Nothing' in Early Christian Thought.* Trans. A. S. Worrall. Edinburgh: T. and T. Clark, 1994.

Mazzarella, Pasquale. "La creazione nel tempor secondo Enrico di Gand." *Discorsi* 2 (1982): 28–40.

McInerny, Ralph. *The Logic of Analogy.* The Hague: Nijhoff, 1961.

McMullin, Ernan. "How Should Cosmology Relate to Theology." In *The Sciences and Theology in the Twentieth Century,* ed. A. R. Peacocke, pp. 17–57. London: Oriel, 1981.

–, ed. *Evolution and Creation.* Notre Dame, Indiana: University of Notre Dame Press, 1985.

Mondolfo, Rodolfo. *L'infinito nel pensiero dell'antichità classica.* Firenze: La Nuova Italia, 1967.

Murdoch, John . "The Condemnation of 1277, God's Absolute Power, and Physical Thought in the Late Middle Ages." *Viator* 10 (1979): 211–244.

Nasr, Seyyed H. *Science and Civilization in Islam.* New York: New American Library, 1970.

Netton, Ian R. *Al-Fārābī and His School.* London and New York: Routledge, 1992.

O'Shaughnessy, Thomas J. *Creation and the Teaching of the Qur'an.* Rome: Biblical Instiute Press, 1985.

Orcibal, Jean. *'In Principio': Interprétations des premiers verses de la Genèse.* Paris: Études Augustiniennes, 1973.

Owens, Joseph. *The Doctrine of Being in the Aristotelian Metaphysics: A Study in the Greek Background of Mediaeval Thought*. 2nd ed. Toronto: Pontifical Institute of Mediaeval Studies, 1963.

–. *An Interpretation of Existence*. Milwaukee, WI: Bruce, 1968.

–. "The Accidental and Essential Character of Being." In *St. Thomas Aquinas on the Existence of God: The Collected Papers of Joseph Owens*, ed. John R. Catan, pp. 52–96. Albany, NY: SUNY Press, 1980.

–. *Towards a Christian Philosophy*. Washington, DC: The Catholic University of America Press, 1990.

Pangallo, Mario. *Il principio di causalità nella metafisica di S. Tommaso*. Roma: Libreria Editrice Vaticano, 1991.

Paulus, Jean. "La Théorie du Premier Moteur chez Aristote." *Revue de Philosophie* 33 (1933): 259–294 and 395–424.

Pearson, Paul. "Creation Through Instruments in Thomas' Sentence Commentary." In *Philosophy and the God of Abraham*, ed. R.J. Long, pp. 147–160.

Pegis, Anton. "A Note on St. Thomas, *Summa Theologica*, I, 44, 1–2." *Mediaeval Studies* 8 (1946): 159–168.

–. "St. Thomas and the Origin of Creation." In *Philosophy and the Modern Mind*, ed. F.X. Canfield, pp. 49–65. Detroit: Sacred Heart Seminary, 1961.

–. *Saint Thomas and the Greeks*. The Aquinas Lecture 1939. Milwaukee, WI: Marquette University Press, 1939.

Philippe, Paul. "Le plan des sentences de Pierre Lombard d'après S. Thomas." *Bulletin thomiste, Notes et communications* 1 (1931–1933): 131*–154*.

Pines, Shlomo. "The Limitations of Human Knowledge according to Al-Fārabī, ibn Bajjah and Maimonides." In *Studies in Medieval Jewish History and Literature*, ed. Isadore Twersky, vol. 1, pp. 82–108. Cambridge: Cambridge University Press, 1979.

–; and Yirmiyahu Yovel, ed. *Maimonides and Philosophy*. Papers presented at the Sixth Jerusalem Philosophical Encounter, May, 1985. Dordrecht: M. Nijhoff, 1986.

–, trans.: *see also* Maimonides.

Polkinghorne, John. "So Finely Tuned a Universe of Atoms, Stars, Quanta, and God." *Commonweal* (16 August 1996): 11–18.

Rahman, Fazlur. "Ibn Sīnā's Theory of the God-World Relationship." In *God and Creation*, ed. D.B. Burrell and B. McGinn, pp. 38–52.

–, ed. and trans.: *see* Avicenna.

Ratzinger, Joseph Cardinal. *'In the Beginning ...': A Catholic Understanding of the Story of Creation and the Fall*. Trans. Boniface Ramsey. Grand Rapids, MI: W.B. Eerdmans, 1995.

Robbins, Frank Egleston. *The Hexaemeral Literature: A Study of the Greek and Latin Commentaries on Genesis*. Chicago: University of Chicago Press, 1912.

Ruello, Francis. "Saint Thomas et Pierre Lombard. Les relations trinitaires et la structure du commentaire des sentences de saint Thomas d'Aquin." *Studi Tomistici* 1, s.d. (1974): 176–209.

Russell, Robert J. "Cosmology from Alpha to Omega." *Zygon* 29 (1994): 557–577.

–; Nancey Murphy; and Arthur Peacocke, ed. *Chaos and Complexity: Scientific Perspectives on Divine Action*. Series on Scientific Perspectives on Divine Action 2. Vatican City: Vatican Observatory Publications, 1995.

Sánchez, Marcelo S. *Aristotele e San Tommaso: un confronto nelle nozioni di assoluto e di materia prima*. Roma: Pontificia Università Lateranense, Città Nuova Editrice, 1981.

Sanguineti, Juan. *La filosofia del cosmo in Tommaso d'Aquino*. Milano: Edizioni Ares, 1986.

Schneider, J.H.J. "Physik und Natur im Kommentar des Thomas von Aquin zur aristotelischen Metaphysik." In *Mensch und Natur im Mittelalter*, ed. A. Zimmermann and A. Speer, 1: 161–192.

Sertillanges, A.D. *L'idée de création et ses retentissements en philosophie*. Paris: Auber, 1945.

Shehadi, Fadlou. *Metaphysics in Islamic Philosophy*. Delmar, NY: Caravan Books, 1982.

Shmuttermayr, Georg. "'Shöpfung aus dem Nichts' in 2 Makk. 7:28?: Zum Verhältnis von Position und Bedeutung," *Biblische Zeitschrift*, neue folge 17 (1973): 203–228.

Smalley, Beryl. *The Study of the Bible in the Middle Ages*. Oxford: Basil Blackwell, 1952. Rept. Notre Dame, IN: University of Notre Dame Press, 1964.

Snyder, Steven. "Albert the Great: Creation and the Eternity of the World." In *Philosophy and the God of Abraham*, ed. R.J. Long, pp. 191–202.

Sokolowski, Robert. *The God of Faith and Reason*. Notre Dame, IN: The University of Notre Dame Press, 1982.

Sorabji, Richard. *Time, Creation, and the Continuum*. Ithaca, N.Y.: Cornell University Press, 1983.

–. "Infinity and the Creation." In *Philoponus and the Rejection of Aristotelian Science*, ed. R. Sorabji, pp. 164–178. Ithaca, NY: Cornell University Press, 1987.

–. *Matter, Space, and Motion: Theories in Antiquity and Their Sequel*. Ithaca, NY: Cornell University Press, 1988.

Torrell, Jean-Pierre. *Initiation à Saint Thomas d'Aquin: Sa personne et son oeuvre*. Paris: Editions Cerf, 1993. Trans. Robert Royal as *Saint Thomas*, vol. 1: *The Person and His Work*. Washington, DC: The Catholic University of America Press, 1996.

Tugwell, Simon, trans. *Albert and Aquinas: Selected Writings*. Classics of Western Spirituality 60. New York: The Paulist Press, 1988.

Urvoy, Dominique. *Ibn Rushd (Averroes)*. Trans. Olivia Stewart. London and New York: Routledge, 1991.

van Steenberghen, Fernand. "La controversie sur l'éternité du monde au XIIIe siècle." *Bulletin de l'Académie Royale de Belgique; Classe des lettres et des sciences morales et politiques* 58 (1972): 141–172.

–. "Le mythe d'un monde éternel." *Revue philosophique de Louvain* 76 (1978): 157–179.

–. *Aristotle in the West: The Origins of Latin Aristotelianism*. 1955. 2nd ed. Louvain: Nauwelaerts; New York: Humanities Press, 1970.

deVaux, Roland. *Notes et texts sur l'Avicennisme latin aux confins des XIIe et XIIIe siècles*. Paris: J. Vrin, 1934.

Vawter, Bruce. "Genesis." In *A New Catholic Commentary on Holy Scripture*, gen. ed. Reginald C. Fuller, pp. 166–205. New York: Thomas Nelson, 1969.

te Velde, Rudi A. *Participation and Substantiality in Thomas Aquinas*. Leiden: E.J. Brill, 1995.

Vollert, Cyril, trans.: *see* Thomas Aquinas.

Wallace, William. "Aquinas on the Temporal Relation between Cause and Effect." *Review of Metaphysics* 27 (1973–74): 569–584.

–. "Aquinas on Creation: Science, Theology, and Matters of Fact." *The Thomist* 38, 3 (1974): 485–523.

–. *The Modeling of Nature: Philosophy of Science and Philosophy of Nature in Synthesis.* Washington, DC: The Catholic University of America Press, 1996.

Ward, Keith. *Religion and Creation.* Oxford: Oxford University Press, 1996.

Weisheipl, James. *Friar Thomas d'Aquino: His Life, Thought, and Works.* New York: Doubleday, 1974. With corrigenda and addenda, Washington, DC: The Catholic University of America Press, 1983.

–. "The Meaning of *Sacra Doctrina* in *Summa theologiae I, q. 1.*" *The Thomist* 38 (1974): 49–80.

–. "The Concept of Nature: Avicenna and Aquinas." In *Thomistic Papers,* ed. Victor B. Brezik, 1 [1984]: 65–82. 6 vols. Houston: Center for Thomistic Studies, University of St. Thomas, 1984–1994.

–. "The Life and Works of St. Albert the Great." In *Albertus Magnus and the Sciences: Commemorative Essays,* ed. Weisheipl, pp. 13–51. Studies and Texts 49. Toronto: Pontifical Institute of Mediaeval Studies, 1980.

–. "The Date and Context of Aquinas' *De aeternitate mundi.*" In *Graceful Reason: Essays in Ancient and Medieval Philosophy Presented to Joseph Owens,* ed. Lloyd Gerson, pp. 239–271. Papers in Mediaeval Studies 4. Toronto: Pontifical Institute of Mediaeval Studies, 1983.

–. *Nature and Motion in the Middle Ages.* Ed. William E. Carroll. Studies in Philosophy and the History of Philosophy 11. Washington, DC: The Catholic University of America Press, 1985.

Wilhelmsen, Frederick D. "Creation as a Relation in Saint Thomas Aquinas." *Modern Schoolman* 56 (1979): 107–133.

Wilks, Ian. "Aquinas on the Past Possibility of the World's Having Existed Forever," *Review of Metaphysics* 48 (1994): 299–329.

Wippel, John F. *The Metaphysical Thought of Godfrey of Fontaines.* Washington, DC: The Catholic University of America Press, 1981.

–. "The Condemnations of 1270 and 1277 at Paris." *Journal of Medieval and Renaissance Studies* 7 (1977): 169–201.

–. "Did Thomas Aquinas Defend the Possibility of an Eternally Created World? (The *De aeternitate mundi* Revisited)." *Journal of the History of Philosophy* 29 (1981): 21–37.

–. "Metaphysics." In *The Cambridge Companion to Aquinas,* eds. Norman Kretzmann and Eleonore Stump, pp. 85–127. Cambridge: Cambridge University Press, 1993.

Wissink, Jozef B., ed. *The Eternity of the World in the Thought of Thomas Aquinas and His Contemporaries.* Studien und Texte zur Geistesgeschichte des Mittelalters 27. Leiden: E.J. Brill, 1990.

Wohlman, Avital. *Thomas d'Aquin et Maïmonide: Un dialogue exemplaire.* Paris: Editions du Cerf, 1988.

Young, M.J.L., J. D. Latham, and R.B. Serjeant, eds. *Religion, Learning and Science in the 'Abbasid Period.* Cambridge History of Arabic Literature. Cambridge: Cambridge University Press, 1990.

Zimmermann, Albert. "*Mundus est aeternus*: Zur Auslegung dieser These bei Bonaventure und Thomas von Aquin." In *Die Auseinandersetzungen an der Pariser Universität in XIII Jahrhundert,* ed. A. Zimmermann, pp. 317–330. Miscellanea Mediaevalia 10. Berlin: Walter de Gruyter, 1976.

–; and Andreas Speer, ed. *Mensch und Natur im Mittelalter.* Miscellanea mediaevalia 21. 2 vols. Berlin: Walter de Gruyter, 1991.

Index